MEET JOHN XXIII

Meet JOHN XXIII

·Joyful Pope and Father to All·

PATRICIA TREECE

SERVANT
BOOKS

PUBLISHED BY ST. ANTHONY MESSENGER PRESS
CINCINNATI, OHIO

Excerpts from the writings of Pope John XXIII used by permission of his literary executor, Monsignor Gianni Carzaniga, Director, Pope John XXIII Foundation. Excerpts from *John XXIII: The Official Biography,* by Mario Benigni and Goffredo Zanzhi, ©2001, Daughters of St. Paul, used by permission of Pauline Books & Media. Excerpts from *Journal of a Soul,* ©1965, used by permission of Continuum International Publishing Group.

Scripture passages have been taken from the *Revised Standard Version,* Catholic edition. Copyright 1946, 1952, 1971 by the Division of Christian Education of the National Council of Churches of Christ in the USA. Used by permission. All rights reserved.

Author's note: Since there are many editions with different page numberings, except where I am quoting the work as given and translated by another author, my quotations and translations from the Italian journal of John XXIII are from *Il Giornale dell'Anima: Soliloqui, note e diari spirituali,* the critical, annotated national edition edited by Alberto Melloni with a national commission of twelve other scholars, four collaborator scholars and others, Instituo per le scienze religiose di Bologna, 1987.

Cover and book design by Mark Sullivan
Cover photo ©Bettmann/CORBIS

LIBRARY OF CONGRESS CATALOGING-IN-PUBLICATION DATA
Treece, Patricia.
Meet John XXIII : joyful pope and father to all / Patricia Treece.
p. cm.
Includes bibliographical references (p.   ).
ISBN 978-0-86716-729-0 (pbk. : alk. paper) 1. John XXIII, Pope, 1881–1963. 2. Popes—Biography. I. Title.
BX1378.2.T69 2008
282.092—dc22
[B]
2008029679

ISBN 978-0-86716-729-0
Copyright ©2008, Patricia Treece. All rights reserved.

Published by Servant Books, an imprint of St. Anthony Messenger Press
28 W. Liberty St.
Cincinnati, OH 45202
www.ServantBooks.org

Printed in the United States of America.

Printed on acid-free paper.

08 09 10 11 12 5 4 3 2 1

With special thanks to
Archbishop Loris Franceso Capovilla,
personal secretary to Pope John XXIII,
whose memories and the documents
—both public and private—
entrusted to him as John's literary executor
form the core of this book.

*These pages are dedicated to
Father Robert Gavotto, O.S.A.,
whose devotion to Pope John XXIII
opened an archbishop's door.*

Contents

. . . . .

Acknowledgments

"I ALWAYS NEEDED THE HELP OF EVERYONE," JOHN BOSCO
said. I echo the saint.

My deep gratitude to my friend Father Robert Gavotto,
O.S.A., who was a seminarian in Rome during John's pontificate: His opening the door to interviews with Archbishop
Loris Francesco Capovilla, Pope John XXIII's personal secretary for his last decade, took this book to its high level of
accuracy and immediacy; his meeting me in Italy to ask my
questions in his elegant, rather than my stumbling, spoken
Italian allowed much more territory to be covered in those
interviews; his transcribing and translating the tapes added
the level of protection possible only when the transcriber
was actually a participant; and his turning a number of my
letters into the polished Italian worthy of an archbishop –
even one as humble as Archbishop Capovilla—was another
blessing. He also has my heartfelt thanks for obtaining the
final crucial permission that permits publication from the

foundation to which the archbishop, now in his nineties, has transferred his rights.

Equally deep is my gratitude to another friend, Francis X. Levy, for his steadfast, devoted help in many areas. This project demanded attribution and permission for every quote. Without his hours of generous, even cheerful labor compiling quotes by source, without his computer expertise and angelic patience during long-distance "bailing out" sessions, without his researching and verifying details and without the security that his backing up my material on his own computer provided, I don't know how I would have survived. Only God can reward Francis for all that unpaid drudgery, but as with Father Gavotto, it is both just and a true joy to thank him publicly. And to thank Mary Levy, my friend and true collaborator through her generous support of her husband's labors and her prayers.

I also owe much to another close friend, Rome-educated (during John's pontificate) scholar-author Father Martinus Cawley, O.C.S.O., of Our Lady of Guadalupe Abbey in Lafayette, Oregon. With unfailing charity he repeatedly made time in his very busy days to share his erudition on Church matters as well as run down elusive information of many kinds, even enlisting his friends, when necessary, on my behalf. To one of them, Father Augustine De Noble, O.S.B., of Mt. Angel Abbey in St. Benedict, Oregon, special thanks for his help on Cardinal Bea.

In the "angelic patience" category, I thank my editor, Cynthia Cavnar of Servant Books, whose spiritual maturity has seen her and me through momentous permission difficulties. Thanks to Lucy Scholand for sharpening my focus in several areas and a clean cut of my 80,000-word manuscript to 50, 000 words.

I thank Archbishop Capovilla for our interviews and, as John's literary executor, for giving me or pointing the way to almost every source used—most of them John's letters, journal or other writings compiled *by* the archbishop or works *on* John done by Capovilla or with his assistance. Almost none available in English, except where noted, the translations from Italian or French are mine and errors my responsibility.

My thanks to the PIME Fathers for permission to quote the interviews with Capovilla by Spanish journalist José Luis González-Balado, which, with revision and amplification by the archbishop himself, make up the PIME publication *Il Cuore di Papa Giovanni*. Gratitude to Sister Piergiovanna Ghezzi, superior of the *Suore delle Poverelle* at Caimaitino, Italy, for information on John's relationship with the order, and to Father Thomas F. Stransky, C.S.P., of the Tantur Biblical Institute in Jerusalem, for information on Giacomo Testa. My thanks to the *Fondazione per le scienze religiose Giovanni XXIII* in Bologna and its Luigia Spaccamonti for books by noted modern historian Giuseppe Alberigo and for photocopying for me John's letters across his lifetime to various women's religious orders, including the *Suore delle Poverelle*.

For research support, special recognition to Ivan Bastoni, Archbishop Capovilla's volunteer secretary, who generously put much time into forwarding questions and answers between me and the archbishop; author Sister Paracleta (Catherine Amrich), SS.C.M.; author and Jewish spirituality expert Rolf Gompertz and the library staff at the Simon Wiesenthal Center in Los Angeles; Bobbie Smith of Livermore, California, for preliminary work; and Doctor

Jennifer Sariego of South Pasadena, California, who tracked down an important supplementary volume of John's letters.

Thanks also to others who helped my communications efforts with Italian sources: production editor Ericka McIntyre of St. Anthony Messenger Press; Marialda Brambilla of Lecco, Italy; Father Kolbe Missionary of the Immaculata; the late Josephine Netherby of Borgo Nuovo, Italy; Kolbe Missionaries Local Directress Anna Brizzi, Ada Locatelli and other Covina, California–based members of that group; and editorial director Lisa Biedenbach for her guidance in one search.

Special gratitude to my friend Maria Angela Collacci and all the *Missionaries di Immacolata Padre Kolbe* of *Via Giovanni XXIII* in Borgo Nuovo, Directress Rafaella Aguzzoni and community, for generously putting me up gratis as well as providing all my Italian transportation with great inconvenience— graciously brushed away—to several members, particularly my last driver, Giovanna Pinotti. Thanks to the Missionaries, this immune-compromised body never climbed aboard any public transport, and I ended my research trip in great shape.

For that and other graces, profound thanks also to all of you who hold me in prayer.

To My Readers

YOU ARE IN FOR A TREAT: "TO KNOW HIM *IS* TO LOVE him." Therefore it is a joy for me to offer you this encounter with the relatively obscure man whose quiet, steady progression in holiness across a long lifetime let him, at age seventy-seven, suddenly become one of the twentieth century's most important figures. "The Good Pope," as even nonbelievers called him, was the catalyst for great changes in the Church and called the world back from the brink of nuclear disaster, among other notable things. There is much for your soul to feed on between these covers, and yet there is still more to say about this saint for our times than I can squeeze in. Look for more books from me on John!

Here, while picturing for you a delightful human being, I also emphasize his ecumenism. I do this not just because certain of Pope John XXIII's historic contributions are fading from public consciousness but also because his *style* in this difficult area models the way that interreligious and interdenominational dialogue must go to save a world drained, equally by hatreds and by pursuits of the trivial, of its God-given potential to be a joyous, mutually accepting human family.

Finally, the heart of this work traces *the ascent to sanctity* of an ambitious, gifted, somewhat proud youth determined to belong fully to God. It highlights the creative responses toward that end that he made time and again to the curves and tragedies life threw at him.

Steeping myself in the life and spirit of John XXIII has been a great gift to this writer, one encouraging me that the call to goodness—even all the way to his heroic charity—is a realistic aspiration for anyone willing to surrender to the Spirit as he did. I hope you end these pages with that same sense.

Beginnings

FROM INFANCY ANGELO GIUSEPPE RONCALLI'S chestnut-colored eyes looked upon the world with placid good humor. As babe grew into child, his regular-featured little face broke easily into smiles, expressing a temperament born for harmony.

If the future pope (what a laugh that suggestion would have raised!) later recalled a few lies, at the time they were committed these filled him with revulsion at himself. Even before Angelino told a cousin that the only thing he wanted was to become a priest, his family and others in their northern Italian village, with its beautiful, mountain-backed, curvy landscape of green fields and treed hills, were affectionately calling the sweet-tempered child *il pretino* ("the little priest").

Does this mean that the boy born November 25, 1881, was a little saint or even a saint in the making? Hardly.

Contrary to the pious view, children who will one day be known as saints more often than not are strong-willed tykes with tendencies to passionate stubbornness, or even aggression, when thwarted. No, if anything, one might have feared that Angelino would be too soft and lacking in inner fire to ever do much spiritually or otherwise. Yet Angelo's life would surprise many, perhaps even him.

FAMILY LIFE

The Roncallis were peasant sharecroppers. Sweet-natured Marianna, Angelo's mother, saw everything in their hard, happy lives in the light of faith. A dedicated family man, community and parish leader, (Giovanni) Battista Roncalli, his father, was equally devout.

Because it took many hands to wrest even a meager living from their small fields in Sotto il Monte ("Under the Mountain"), Angelo's hardworking parents lived with some of Battista's uncles, an aunt and a cousin—the whole family under the headship of the oldest resident male, Battista's Uncle Zaverio.

Retired Archbishop Loris Capovilla, who would be Angelo Roncalli's secretary as pope, knew (and still knows) the Roncalli family well. He estimated that as many as thirty-two people lived in the big stucco house, with its long second-floor balcony, that was part of the sharecropping arrangement. The archbishop writes: "Living in this crowded space lacking so many necessities [all these people] shared rooms that were suffocating in summer and cold in winter with cows housed as were the silkworms [a major cash crop] near the kitchen. The old folks [were] set closest to the fire, and the squalls of the newborn were heard twice a year or there·abouts."[1]

Marianna would rear ten living children, losing her first child, Caterina, when Angelo—her first son and fourth-born—was a toddler. She would lose several others later. Battista's cousin's wife would also have ten children who lived to be play-mates of Angelo. Little wonder that the eldest boy of twenty children in one house would be a convivial soul. Thinking of all these impoverished sharecroppers jammed up together, Capovilla summed up: "[Such a life] is a difficult art that one may well pro-pose requires men [and women] who are truly magnanimous!"[2]

And magnanimous they were. When all these people gathered to eat, their food was polenta or minestrone. They were too poor, Angelo would later reminisce, to have bread. As for cake or meat, slivers of such fabled foods appeared rarely, Angelo recalling slices of homemade cake only on Christmas and Easter. Yet he also remembered: "Nevertheless when a beggar appeared at our kitchen door where twenty children waited impatiently for their scoop of minestrone, my mother hurried to seat him among us."[3]

And he noted how well family members treated each other, including the two unrelated wives who shared a kitchen and household chores. Recalling his lively, happy home, where people tried to live in true Christian harmony in spite of a poverty that limited food, reserved shoes for church and dictated that each piece of clothing last "years and years," all his life Angelo would treasure the "precious teaching" of that place. "I have forgotten much of what I have learned from books," he wrote years later, "but I recall still, blessedly, all I learned from my parents and [household] elders."[4]

3

DEDICATED TO GOD

His godfather, Great-Uncle Zaverio—a saintly man whose profound spiritual influence on Angelo is commemorated by a plaque at the future pope's birthplace—dedicated Angelo at baptism to Jesus' Sacred Heart. And Angelo's first memory was of his mother telling him that she had dedicated him to Jesus' mother, Mary. Such devout people accepted his desire to be a priest. Zaverio, Battista and Marianna made the sacrifice of the labor this son could have contributed *and* his future headship as the eldest male of his generation.

Somehow they found the money to have Angelo tutored, first in Italian (the family spoke a Bergamesque dialect) and then in Latin. Another saintly man, the village pastor, got eleven-year-old Angelo into the minor seminary in 1892 on a trial basis. He and one of the Roncallis' four brother landlords, this one a priest, came up with the fees. The boy would secretly always suffer from homesickness, but after a rocky start scholastically, he did well.

Particularly during his fourteenth year, Angelo seemed to take flight both in his study and in his spiritual formation.[5] At the suggestion of his spiritual director, the young student began the notebooks of reflections, self-examinations, spiritual and human resolutions, remembrances of his life and moving words from others that have proved inspirational to millions under the title *Journal of a Soul*. He also began to anchor himself in various spiritual families and associations whose spiritual wisdom would strengthen his ties to God and the Church. Each required periods of spiritual preparation and study, and each added its flavor to his spirituality.

4

Through Zaverio he was a lay member, called a cooperator, in later-canonized Father John Bosco's Salesian works for the young, with a spirituality that emphasizes cheerfulness in serving God and humanity. The Salesians teach how to lead others spiritually through one's availability and complete self-giving in a kindly, reasonable style, which makes both the bearer of these good things and religion itself loved. Down the years, Angelo would talk less of the Salesians than of the Franciscans, but phrases straight from Don Bosco would turn up in his mouth and in his writing. In particular he would later use the saint's motto, "Give me souls; take all the rest," to express his own aspirations.[6]

At the seminary he became a novice in the institution's Marian confraternity, a spirituality with a self-discerning Jesuit flavor but even more indebted to the saint for whom Bosco named *his* order, master of good cheer Saint Francis de Sales. The confraternity emphasized de Sales's "gentleness, zeal and surrender to God."[7]

THE FRANCISCAN

Finally, Angelo became a third order (lay member) Franciscan. This spiritual family of the Church would be a great bulwark to someone who would always be poor materially, helping him come to regard his poverty and that of his family as a treasure. Franciscan priests, brothers and sisters take vows of poverty. Lay Franciscans take no vow but try to live simply.

As a seminarian Angelo lived more than simply. Only two years before ordination his *Journal* notes, "Since I became a seminarian, I have never worn a piece of clothing that was not given me by the charity of some kind person."[8] The Roncallis' poverty meant that everything else, from fees to textbooks, had to come the same way.

As a diocesan priest Angelo would vow chastity and obedience to Church superiors but take no vow of poverty. By inheritance or investment, there are rich diocesan priests. (It's expected that their money will be used for good and that the priest's lifestyle will be in keeping with his calling.) Angelo would *appear* to rise from his childhood poverty to affluence when seen years later officiating in the rich vestments of a cardinal or chauffeured along the streets of Europe in a luxury sedan. Such sights were illusion: He never rose from poverty, nor would he have seen riches as *rising* in his case.

Not that Angelo Roncalli acquired romantic notions of poverty. Writing home as a bishop years later, he expressed sorrow that the family's little ones must suffer so from the cold during winter. From the winters of his own childhood, he added, he still had physical marks on his hands. (Called chilblains, these are inflammation and swelling of hands or feet, accompanied by itching and a hot sensation. Severe cases develop ulcers). In later years so much of his churchman's stipend went to help others that there would never be much for himself. He felt bad about that only when he had nothing left to give those who approached him with extended hands. He wrote in one letter during the winter of 1934, "[There is] great misery around me; even greater...is my sorrow at not being able to lift it."[9]

Still, to be poor was how "the son of Providence," as he came to term himself, wanted it.[10] For others it was another story: He would bemoan poverty that crushed lives and do what he could to lift it.

WHAT ABOUT SEXUALITY?

Angelo was born in an era when the virtue of modesty was highly praised. Human sexuality, however, was as natural a part of peasant life as the cows' being bred so the family would have milk or roosters' mounting hens in the yard. The relationships of Angelo's parents and of Battista's cousins, Luigi and Angela, were marked not just by modesty and fidelity but by a fecundity that made it plain nobody was stinting on sex.

At the same time the other five adult members of the household lived as celibates. Celibacy was as acceptable as the married state, many households in Europe and the Americas profiting from the extra hands of bachelor uncles and maiden aunts. Of Angelo's ten siblings to reach adulthood, five would marry, and five remain lifelong celibates.

In such an atmosphere Angelo could hardly believe that celibacy required superhuman effort and was next to impossible. That doesn't mean he was spared powerful sexual urges. He began mentioning sexual temptation in his journal when he was about fifteen years old. At the age of twenty he wrote, "Is my flesh bronze?"[11] fearful he would betray his ideals.

But *Journal* entries also show he dealt with his drives successfully in time-honored ways: self-distraction, "careful watch over my eyes" on walks in the city,[12] consideration of Jesus' life and sufferings, self-reminders that an angel of God was beside him and should never be offended by his deeds, remembrance of the judgment at death, quick invocations to his guardian angel or to the Mother of Jesus to pray for him and the practical safeguard of going to bed with a rosary round his neck and keeping his arms crossed on his chest all night.[13]

The youth's sleep preparations, however laughable some may find them, were effective because they originated from the profound desire to channel the power of his sexuality into generating spiritual force. Or as he put it in his *Journal*:

> [One can't] deny the impressions of the senses or the calls of nature. [They exist but] the taste of God's love, the sweet and total abandonment to his will, must absorb everything else in me, or better put, transform and sublimate all that comes from those lower parts of myself.[14]

This was especially true after Angelo's realization—which grew ever sharper during his seminary years—that Jesus wanted from him not just a mediocre but the highest morality. In 1902 he expanded the insight: "From signs received, and from the wonderful graces which God has poured into my soul, from my childhood until now, it is quite obvious that, for his own adorable purposes, he wants to make me entirely holy."[15]

Angelo—like his mentors, lay and clerical—would settle for nothing less than purity, that state involving the entire being of a person in which the sexual aspect, healthily sublimated and transcendent in those called to celibacy, generates the joyous, pure *agape* love called charity. He wrote: "A globe of purest crystal… that is how I see the purity of the priest's heart."[16]

Observers felt he attained that lofty goal, while he himself expressed gratitude in his last days that he had never given in to sexual temptation.

OF SIN AND HEROIC VIRTUE

He did not want to give in to other temptations either. On a February retreat in 1900, Angelo made a vow that with God's help he would never sin deliberately. A quarter-century later he thanked God in his journal for the graces to have kept that vow, this graced state continuing, according to Archbishop Capovilla—who was beside him the last decade of Angelo's life—all the way to a holy death.

Let there be no confusion. In no way does this mean that Angelo was perfect, a human being without fault. In 1900 he still faced years of sharp struggle against his involuntary human weaknesses, but the many slips he made were not *deliberate* decisions to do what he knew at that moment was wrong.

An example: Angelo talked too much. When not carried away in his jabbering—and he *was* often carried away in youth's impetuousness—he experienced self-aware moments of choice. This led to waging interior battles again and again to stop himself from sharing bits of gossip burning on his tongue; he learned, too, to kill, not just once but over and over, those comments that subtly showed his intellectual superiority or how shabbily he felt he was being treated.

Deliberately given in to, these are the behaviors the Church terms venial sins, as opposed to those termed mortal because they get a stranglehold on the soul. In not giving in whenever he was conscious—and consciousness over the years eventually became habitual—as days turned into years of struggle Angelo slowly developed the heroic virtue of the saint he felt called to be. This even as he complained in his journal about his failings and lack of virtue.

9

In a letter to the seminary, Angelo's pastor had predicted "great things" for the boy. Others concurred. He received a scholarship to finish his training in Rome.[17] As is still true today, seminarians receiving this select education knew some of their classmates would become Church leaders.

❧ 2 ❧

Formation in Rome

ANGELO'S FIRST LETTER HOME, IN JANUARY 1901, WAS ALL excitement and approval:

> The Lord could not have blessed me more...nor could I imagine better fortune.... As for my health, I'm doing wonderfully.... I received the warmest welcome imaginable [and]...I've found excellent companions....
>
> I am not at all bothered by classes and study; actually, I'm enjoying myself. Even regarding piety, it is possible to do one's own practices very well....
>
> In our chapel one venerates a most beautiful image of Our Lady of Confidence. I recommend you to her [asking Mary's prayers] every morning and evening.

He described his narrow, poorly lit room, with its limited air supply from one small, grated window, as "a beautiful room to myself with a nice bed—a bit too hard truthfully but that will do me a lot of good…. [There is] every comfort: a chest of drawers, a little table, a high-backed chair, a bookshelf, etc."

The kindness of Sotto il Monte's assistant pastor had sent Angelo to Rome for the first time the previous year, on pilgrimage for the 1900 Holy Year. Living there, however, offered so much more:

> Every day I go for a walk, so I am able to visit many holy places and pray for you and for me…. I can't tell you all the wonders you can see here.
>
> The other night, for example, I was at an academy… [for those from missionary areas]. I listened to forty clerics who had completed their studies present their papers—in forty different languages…. If you could have seen it! There were people of every color…!
> …And the pope? I was already able to see him on Sunday evening in St. Peter's…. I got close enough to get a good look…and receive his blessing.[1]

It was just icing on the cake that in June of 1901 Angelo received his degree in theology, with an award for proficiency in Hebrew.

OF MILITARY MATTERS

That November his next-younger brother was called up for military service. The Roncallis could not spare a second son from the fields, so Angelo agreed to take his brother's place. For a year, until November 1902, he exchanged his seminary cassock for an infantryman's uniform.

In spite of prevalent anticlericalism, the seminarian with the sweet smile was well liked. His commanding officers promoted him to corporal in May and to sergeant at the end of his service period. As pope he would write that he had cherished the experience "of getting to know the souls of the young sons of Italy, and of finding out the best practical ways of drawing them to all that is good [at the summits of]... Christian feeling and living."[2]

True, but in spite of his sense that God was always heaping blessings on him, such as his nightly meetings with his old Bergamo rector and unsought special treatment from other soldiers won over by his goodness, emotional *Journal* entries immediately after his service reveal an innocent's "year of conflicts." He wrote of the barracks, "What blasphemies there were in that place, and what filth!"[3] By filth he meant lewd sexual talk.

On December 31, looking back over the year, his entry states:

> [thanks God] with all my heart.... I might, like so many other poor wretches, have lost my vocation.... I might have lost holy purity and the grace of God, but God did not allow...this. I passed through the mire and by his grace I was kept unpolluted. I am still alive, healthy, robust..., better than before.[4]

As for the infantrymen, mostly "poor wretches, who grew up surrounded by evil,"[5] he had enough sense to realize that they might be more blameless before God than he, who had the moral advantages of a devout home.

He would bring much more maturity to his next military service and consequently much less fear of being sucked into sin.

A SPIRITUAL MASTER

Safely out of "that awful military uniform,"[6] Angelo was assigned a new confessor-director as guide through the last stages of seminary psycho-spiritual formation. From the moment Angelo looked into the kindly face of frail Redemptorist Francesco Pitocchi, he felt complete confidence in baring his soul to one whose reputation was that of a true spiritual master. Angelo would seek Pitocchi's counsel when possible in post-seminary years and say of him at his death in June 1922:

> How charity...[shone]...throughout the entire person of Don Francesco! To approach him, open one's heart and feel the heartfelt warmth of his fatherly tenderness, would take but an instant. His goodness was...(the patience of Christ), endlessly bearing the weight of our troubles and indiscretions.[7]

Pitocchi saw fertile ground in Angelo, agreeing with the seminary leadership that here was a seminarian in whom seeds of holiness might be sown. On his first retreat under Pitocchi in 1902, Angelo made an honest catalogue of his failings. Like everyone committed to getting beyond innate human egotism to surrender to God, the twenty-one-year-old confronted with chagrin plenty of imperfections. Referring to the major fault "self-love" with its "spirit of pride, presumption and vanity," he also listed pride again as "arrogance" before going on to "negligence in my duties," and "infinite distractions." "Vanity," he detailed, [was a foe] "in my thoughts, words and deeds." "I think of lording it over others, making a name for myself, displaying my powers," "strutting about like a professor," "the shade of envy always in my thoughts."[8]

At the same time he experienced the truth that God did not condemn him. Instead Jesus showed him "the affection of a loving mother," and he recognized more fully his own love for Jesus.[9]

But loving and being loved did not vanquish failings overnight. Father Pitocchi counseled: "Always obey, with simplicity and good nature, and leave everything to the Lord."[10] Obedience without question or complaint would one day be a hallmark of Angelo Roncalli. But when he was given the job of taking care of the seminary's sickroom inhabitants, he wrote honestly that the task was one "I find humiliating, and which offends my pride. It costs me an enormous sacrifice to obey." Then he added, "Well then, let us obey; let us pluck up our courage and be cheerful in the Lord."[11] And obey cheerfully he did.

THE STRUGGLE: PRIDE

Struggle is the exercise that builds psycho-spiritual muscle. One measure of the strength Angelo developed is the fact that he is known today for virtues whose opposites he so often felt he battled unsuccessfully throughout his student years.

Most of his involuntary failings were those one might expect of a firstborn son in a culture that made him "special" as the next head of the family. Singled out by family head Zaverio, he also had looking up to him the residential horde of peers—sisters, brothers and cousins. If his temperament was sweet like his mother's, it was also made for leadership like his father's. Consequently, however amiable he was, or at least desired to be, young Angelo had opinions on almost everything and the disposition to express them freely.

The sort of youth whose hand was always up in class, he always had something to say, wherever he was. He thought he knew what others ought to do, too, and told them, describing himself unsparingly as "wanting to be a Solomon, to sit in judgment, to lay down the law left and right!"[12]

He even found himself being a know-it-all with those to whom he was expected to defer in judgment. A *Journal* entry for September 1, 1900, laments that more than once with a group of ordained priests in Bergamo he had "allow[ed] myself to hold forth as an authority about politics, airing my opinions about this and that, one question after another—in short, flinging myself into the discussion in a way unsuitable" for one not yet even ordained.[13]

Even in his final seminary days, the *Journal* bemoans "heated arguments," probably with peers, when others disagreed with his views.[14]

At home too, on vacation from the seminary, he ran into trouble in 1898 with what some locals considered arrogance. Part of this was his overly exalted conception of how he had to behave in order to uphold priestly dignity. (He might learn to be amiable and approachable by all, but concern with dignity as Christ's priest would always be part of his personality.) As late as 1900 this led him to refuse to join in the chitchat in the kitchen, an action that his bewildered family apparently took as being uppity.

He even was told off once that year by his long-suffering

mother. Her criticism devastated him as no other's could—even the occasional whisper that he wanted to become a priest to avoid labor in the fields—since whatever adolescent stupidity his pursuit of clerical dignity evoked, he loved his mother deeply.

Years later he confided to Capovilla that his seminary, academic and personal achievements, which put him so much in the light and at the top of whatever group of students he was in, were not motivated entirely by his genuine desire to be "a priest, in the service of simple souls."[15] Besides altruistic motivations, he had a true love of learning. And ambition was involved. He studied obsessively, ardently wanting to be like certain churchmen revered even beyond the Church for knowledge in almost every known field. Such men, Angelo believed, brought souls to Christ and honor to the Church.

He daydreamed frequently during class or in church of the great things he would accomplish. Even when he was serving at the altar his attention sometimes wandered.

Two Unusual Strengths

A trait that helped counter ambition and all the other manifestations of ego Angelo struggled with was his unusual self-honesty. He swept none of his faults under the rugs of denial or excuse. As early in his seminary career as 1897, when he was only fifteen or sixteen, he noted, "I who always criticize others" botched his part so badly in a seminary Mass—daydreaming?—that "everyone laughed at me, and I deserved it."[16]

His spiritual director listened with a compassionate ear to Angelo's honest admission of frequent lapses into his various failings, but his experienced eye took in Angelo's sincere love of God and determination to surrender to divine love. Pitocchi also saw a second unusual trait of this seminarian: an innate balance. In all his spiritual work, Angelo was greatly helped by a personality not prone to extremes. His self-castigations were mentally healthy and reality based, not overly exaggerated or seriously scrupulous. For instance, when he journaled about his "excessive mirth," he noted, "But, after all, it is always better to be merry than to be melancholy."[17] If he was egotistical and ambitious, as are so many youths, these traits were countered by insight into them as forms of pride he was determined to conquer to be entirely Christ's man.

Pitocchi offered healing medicine in the meditation and mantra, "God is all; I am nothing."[18] As time went on, the Redemptorist customized three foundations for Angelo's spiritual progress: "the way of humility, union with God and obedience in all my doings to the will of God and not to my own will."[19]

Under this wise direction Angelo slowly interiorized what he heard so often: Gifts are gifts from God (see 1 Corinthians 4:7–8), so why be proud? A really successful priest in spiritual terms, he began to grasp, is ambitious for *God's* work, not his own. In 1903, his last year of seminary studies, he acknowledged: "We think we cannot be really great men unless we are supremely learned. But this is to use the same standards as the world, and we must get used to taking a different view. My real greatness lies in doing the will of God, entirely and perfectly."[20]

Retreating ego would still trip Angelo up now and then. Urged by Pitocchi four months after ordination to give a little talk to a Marian group that met under the holy

Redemptorist's direction, Roncalli "wrote everything down...
[doing] my best to weave a flowery garland of praise for our
dear heavenly Mother.... It was too studied, too flowery, too
poetical." Facing real people and suddenly feeling a country
bumpkin, "I lost my presence of mind, my fluency, my
fervour; I even lost my way in my own manuscript."

In short, the talk was a "complete failure." Pitocchi consoled him "with words of such persevering kindness, that in
the end" Angelo could actually journal, "I was content to have
suffered that mortification."[21]

The fiasco revealed that in spite of all he knew *about*
God—by this time he had a doctorate in theology—the relationship needed growth. But the event was a watershed. In
psychological terms, after this incident Angelo became his
own consoling mentor. For the rest of his life, similar attitudes
toward faux pas and failures evidenced a rare and graced
capacity for creatively turning painful experiences into psychological and spiritual growth. In mystical terms, egotism had
received a fatal blow: The humiliations that lay ahead, under
the Holy Spirit's guidance, without implying inhuman perfection, would be ladder rungs on Angelo's ascent to sanctity.

ORDINATIONS: SUBDIACONATE, DIACONATE AND PRIESTLY

Thanks to the progress made under Pitocchi, Angelo was
some paces down the narrow path to spiritual maturity when,
in April 1903, at St. John Lateran—burning with love for
Christ and ready to vow lifelong chastity—he was ordained a
subdeacon. His *Journal* entry about the occasion will echo
down the years prophetically:

When, after the solemn prostration, I approached the altar, and the Cardinal, accepting my vow, robed me in my new and glorious habit, it seemed to me that the Popes, confessors and martyrs who sleep in their silent tombs in the great basilica arose and embraced me like brothers, rejoicing with me and joining in the chorus of the Resurrection angels to praise Jesus who in all his glory has deigned to raise such an unworthy creature to so great a height.[22]

In December Angelo was ordained a deacon. Eight months later his priestly ordination followed the usual pattern: a nine-day retreat, reception of the sacrament of ordination and first Masses, including one on a visit home.

The retreat, to which the twenty-two-year-old brought intense fervor—in a room close to that in which the founder of the Passionists, Saint Paul of the Cross, had died—was at that order's venerable house on Rome's Caelian Hill. The house is at the center of the Church in a sense, for, as Angelo noted, from its windows many of the most important sites of Christianity are visible.

Ordination took place early on the morning of August 10, 1904, in Santa Maria in Monte Santo Church, located in the Piazza del Popolo, the "people's plaza." During the rite he felt Christ's mother smiling at him. That afternoon he went alone on foot to visit certain images of her and places associated with other favorite saints:

I visited St Philip Neri, St Ignatius, St John Baptist de Rossi, St Aloysius, St John Berchmans, St Catherine of Siena, St Camillus de Lellis and many others. O blessed

saints, who...were witnesses to the Lord [see Hebrews
12:1] of my good intentions,...ask him to forgive my
weaknesses and to help me to keep ever alight in my
heart the flame of that...day.[23]

The coming December he would remind his saintly great-
uncle, "The priest is made but that's not enough; we want a
holy priest who will do great good to all." And he would ask
Zaverio's prayers for "great humility and apostolic zeal."[24]

The morning after his ordination, Angelo had the
longed-for privilege of saying his first Mass by the tomb of
Saint Peter. He wrote, "I said to the Lord over the tomb
...(Peter's words): 'Lord, you know everything; you know
that I love you' [John 21:17]. I came out from the church as if
in a dream."[25]

His vice-rector had arranged a papal audience for mid-
day. Peter's successor, Pope Pius X, born a peasant boy himself, was more than gracious and included a blessing for "all
the people who are rejoicing at this time for your sake."[26]

His second Mass was at the summer quarters of his seminary. Don Pitocchi, giving the homily, the *Journal* notes, was
"too kind in what he said about me: his affection blinded him
a little."[27] That humble notation spoke volumes about God's
work, through Pitocchi and other means, in Angelo Roncalli.

Heading for home, he said his third Mass in Florence, to
thank Our Lady for her prayer help in maintaining purity
during military service and his fourth in Milan at the tomb of
a heavenly friend and role model, Saint Charles Borromeo
(see 1 Corinthians 4:16; Philippians 3:17; 1 Thessalonians 1:6).
From Angelo's tenth year, he had been drawn to this

northern Italian cardinal archbishop, a largehearted, great Church reformer. "How much I had to tell him!" he wrote in his *Journal*, adding that since that Mass, "the veneration and love which bind me to him have grown stronger."[28]

Then the new *Don* Roncalli came at last to humble Sotto il Monte. Carrying the great gift of Pius's blessing on them all for his joyous first home Mass—to be said that very day, the Feast of the Assumption—he was greeted not just by his ecstatic parents, Zaverio and the other relations but by the whole village. Years since there had been a newly ordained among them, bells ringing, they led him under triumphal arches, with rejoicing and strewing of flowers, as if he had been a bishop.[29]

❧ 3 ❧

A Priest of Bergamo

IN OCTOBER 1904 THE NEW DON ANGELO RONCALLI WAS back in Rome. Rather than being assigned to a parish, he had been sent to take a three-year course in canon law.

Then the gentle bishop of Bergamo died. Early in 1905 a well-known and popular sociology professor at Rome's Collegio Leoniano—a priest Don Angelo considered one of "the most outstanding"—was selected to replace him. In a letter Angelo was profuse in praise of Giacomo Maria Radini Tedeschi's "piety, his vast and profound learning,...his innumerable and worthy... relationships and connections,...affable manner...and above all his apostolic zeal."[1]

Wonder of wonders, suddenly young Don Roncalli was told to close his barely opened canon law textbooks. Because he was from Bergamo, yet was one of the few available young priests with the breadth of a Roman education, he, twenty-three-year-old Angelo Roncalli, had been chosen by the distinguished new bishop as his secretary. Don Roncalli even participated in Radini Tedeschi's consecration ceremony in the Sistine Chapel, honored to hold the Gospels over the man's head.

WIDER, EVER WIDER

If Roman education had broadened Angelo Roncalli, his assignments under this vigorous new bishop would widen his views and understanding immensely more. As secretary, he lived in Radini Tedeschi's household, seeing up close an outstanding bishop's spiritual practices, duties and innovations. Radini Tedeschi was a great organizer and, as his secretary would later write in a biography of the formidable man, someone who wanted to carry the Church forward, maintaining its "glorious traditions" but "in harmony with the new conditions and needs of the time."[2]

This meant many things. Physical properties of the Church, such as ramshackle rectories, were replaced. Others were brought up to date. For instance, heating was added to the seminary, where for several centuries half-frozen boys, including Angelo, had huddled, clothes on, under the bedcovers in icy dormitories.

Catholic Action, with its varied apostolates carried out by laity for laity, in union with the area bishop, was already established in Bergamo in Roncalli's childhood. Under Radini Tedeschi it was promoted even more vigorously on behalf of labor, peasant farmers—and women. And there was much more tradition-respecting innovation, all involving, it seems, tasks for the secretary. This arduous schedule meant it was not that often, to his regret, that he could find free time to visit his family. He might chide himself in his 1907 retreat notes that he had not learned to make the best use of time, but in fact he was working incessantly.[3] And the pleasant manner he brought to all these tasks won him many admirers and friends, among these Radini Tedeschi, who became another, and many think the greatest, of his spiritual fathers. For the rest of his life, Don Angelo would reflect the importance of this relationship by referring, even as pope, to Giacomo Maria Radini Tedeschi simply as "my bishop."

With a bishop of this kind, there was lots of travel. Locally Roncalli accompanied Radini Tedeschi on pastoral visitations of every one of the 352 churches in the diocese. That took from December 1905 until 1909. Nationally there were many trips to Rome and to Italian cities new to Don Angelo, all the way south to Naples.

In April 1905 "the bishop's shadow," as his secretary was called, followed Radini Tedeschi out of Italy to Lourdes—Angelo's first of many spiritually enriching visits—with stops at other important French shrines. His 1906 retreat was replaced by a moving diocesan pilgrimage with the bishop to the Holy Land; in 1908 he was at Lourdes again; 1911 brought time in Switzerland and various new French cities; in 1912 he discovered Austria, Poland and Hungary. Only in 1913 did the bishop's health troubles stop this culturally and spiritually widening exposure to new lands, new languages, new people.

NEW TASKS, NEW PEOPLE

After passing half his life as a student, Roncalli was asked to add teaching to his secretarial duties. Wanting to do some inconspicuous reform, the new bishop handed his secretary the additional delicate assignment to be "spokesperson for the seminarians on one hand, and on the other, for the members of the disciplinary commission."[4] This meant learning to work on committees (over the next few years at the seminary and elsewhere there would be lots of them) and learning to bring disputants together.

Professor Roncalli first taught Church history, then apologetics and patrology. With no teaching experience, he was too intimidated or too busy the first year to do more than read the textbook to the class. His teaching was consequently considered, understating it, "rather monotonous." Then he got into his stride, and his classes became the seminary's "most popular."[5]

Don Roncalli's job as secretary, he noted in his journal, "demands the greatest tact and prudence"[6] interacting with many people. Because his bishop was involved beyond the diocese, young Roncalli also made these broadening contacts, including, as early as December 1905, an edifying and exciting relationship with Cardinal Andrea Ferrari of Milan. Angelo had been only thirteen when, as part of a pilgrimage to a Eucharistic Congress in Milan, Ferrari's observable extraordinary devotion to the Eucharist and his ardent commentary on John 15:9's admonition to love had left the boy with the awed impression he had seen a saint. Of Ferrari, Don Angelo eventually wrote in his diary, "He envelops me with so much kindness that it is almost embarrassing."[7]

Beginning in 1908, Achille Ratti, of Milan's Ambrosian Library, lent help to the younger priest's research on Roncalli's favorite saint, Milan's Cardinal Archbishop Saint Charles Borromeo. Achille Ratti would become Pope Pius XI in 1922.

Don Angelo also made friends with peers, the up-and-coming men who were secretaries to people like Ferrari. And in 1910 he befriended a younger man, a new teacher of biblical science at the seminary. Don Gustavo Testa, ordained in Bergamo that year by Radini Tedeschi, was returning from study in Rome. The two forged lifelong ties before Testa was summoned to Rome in 1920 for diplomatic training. From far-flung places or less often in close proximity, the knot of their friendship would never loosen—as evidenced by the fact that in 1959, Don Roncalli, as pope, would make Gustavo Testa a cardinal.

BEGINNING TO SHINE

His PH.D. in theology, Roncalli began teaching with only a general knowledge of Church history, a topic he discovered fascinating. And knowing the history of the Church in more depth, especially adding deeper study of the Church fathers for the patrology class, proved another important broadening experience.

At the bishop's request, in 1907 Don Angelo gave a deeply researched, very successful historical lecture on a late cardinal of local interest, which the local paper praised as "timely, concise, brilliant."[8] The proud bishop had his spiritual son's lecture published in a scholarly Milan review. As for Roncalli, he found spiritual benefits from contact with "vast horizons illuminated by... truth and sanctity."[9]

It was the start of various historical research projects and publications, including in 1909 the one on Saint Charles Borromeo, which, limited to his spare time, would take nearly a lifetime. Soon, whenever there was to be some special commemoration of Bergamo's ecclesiastical past, Don Roncalli was called to produce publications or lectures for the occasion. All these projects resulted in the extremely important ability—looking at past reforms, for instance—"to make appropriate comparisons with the present times."[10]

As early as the 1906 Holy Land pilgrimage, Don Roncalli revealed another talent, writing articles with vivid descriptions of people and places for Bergamo's press. That same year Radini Tedeschi started a monthly diocesan bulletin for priests. With his approval, in 1909 Don Roncalli changed the format of *La Vita Diocesana* to one providing ongoing education of the diocesan clergy. With the help of one other person, each month Don Angelo personally wrote the thirty-six pages, including meaty items like his series profiling the diocese's past bishops. As he would remark in old age, his was becoming a life passed "pen in hand."[11]

After the hugely successful lecture in 1907, Don Roncalli was in demand as a speaker around the diocese. Preparing these talks took time from one who had none. During his 1908 retreat he noted, "The numerous tasks assigned to me leave my head and heart in a ferment of excitement and prevent my attending seriously and whole-heartedly to anything." And on the 1909 retreat he confessed, "All the things I have to do...confuse my brain."[12]

Thus he once arrived to give a talk and couldn't recall a word. Understandably, said the young orator, giving talks sometimes led to real feelings of fear. But he must have done well, for the invitations kept coming.

In the summer of 1907, in order that Roncalli not be recalled to military service, the bishop made him interim pastor of a small church, Santa Maria d'Oleno, whose pastor had just died. The holiness of his pastor back in Sotto il Monte had caused Roncalli wholesome reflections as a seminarian. This July-to-November pastorate replowed that same furrow: He saw the goodness of humble people only too willing to cooperate with a priest who extended them a little pastoral kindness and goodwill. Again he realized the spiritual potential of being a simple pastor for simple folk.

He may have felt the occasional prick of shards of pride, with its ambition to do great things, but his retreat notes of 1909 show that he had gotten a stranglehold on letting that part of his personality direct any of his acts. To practice humility and deliberately further squash his ego, he joined a newly revived diocesan religious order, begun with only four men by Radini Tedeschi, the Congregation of the Priests of the Sacred Heart. He noted: "Being a member of the new Congregation...will place me under a stricter obligation not to be self-seeking in any way, but always to follow the will of God as expressed in the will of my Bishop."[13]

A FRIEND OF WOMEN

Laymen in the Bergamo diocese, including Roncalli's father and great-uncle, had been notably and commendably active in initiatives of Catholic Action and other politico-social undertakings, while their women stayed voiceless at home. But women's lives were changing. As a former sociology professor, Radini Tedeschi understood this and greatly favored social initiatives for women. So it was perhaps natural to the bishop that Don Roncalli be active in this arena too.

Starting in November 1907 the busy priest shoehorned into his schedule teaching in Catholic Action's School of Religion for young women schoolteachers and other women who wanted to teach religion in elementary schools. Three locations in the city eventually existed, and for several years Don Roncalli taught all the classes in each.

Apparently he had a particular gift for apostolic collaboration, not just with laity but with women laity. In 1910 local women petitioned the bishop to have Don Roncalli as priest assistant to Bergamo's newly established local chapter of the Union of Catholic Women, founded by women from the local Catholic Society of Mutual Aid. Without ceasing to give the School of Religion teachers' weekly religion classes, he now was finding themes for this second group's weekly meetings, locating their guest speakers, organizing their retreats and other spiritual activities, as well as promoting the new organization to the diocesan pastors—women not seen as capable of doing these things for themselves.

Another load for the willing back: He was asked to take on a Women's Education Club, which—with a lot of his hard work—benefited many as a sort of public university.

All these enterprises added up to a lot of time with women, many of whom were not only devout but also young and appealing. He was young, good-looking and kind, assuring he was appealing too. Later he would look back on the sexual temptations he faced in those early years and say he was glad for the quieting down of his sexual urges. But already in his Bergamo days, Don Roncalli was no longer the youth scared of his sexuality.

He was guided safely through sexual temptations by the

resolve found in his journal, "that my behavior shall always be kind, modest and dignified so as to divert attention from my own person and give a richer spiritual quality to my work." And referring specifically to his commitment to purity, he noted: "It would be dangerous if in this work I were to presume on my own powers." Instead he would "raise my thoughts constantly to Jesus, returning to his embrace as soon as I have ended my task."[14]

He kept up these precautions even with women vowed to chastity. And there were lots of religious sisters in his life because perhaps no one appreciates an outstanding priest better than they. In Bergamo's convents, whether to say Mass, teach their recruits, give retreats or collaborate in work for young girls, Don Roncalli was in demand.

As a boy he used to look at the photos, in a double frame hanging on the wall of his pastor's rectory, of a sister superior (today beatified) and a priest who were cofounders of the Daughters of the Sacred Heart in Bergamo. Don Roncalli met the Daughters in 1905 while accompanying Radini Tedeschi on the bishop's first round of convent visits in Bergamo. From this grew a long, fruitful association. The sisters' 1906–1914 annals record many homilies and conferences by Don Angelo for the young girls who were this group's apostolate. Moreover, from 1915 to 1921, good Don Roncalli was summoned to preside for all the feasts dearest to the community itself.

Later, when he was no longer simple Don Roncalli, he kept up the relationship with the group and won the Daughters' hearts forever by his help from afar with the biography of their foundress.

There was a second group of sisters who became so close to Roncalli that, in the last nine years of his life, they would form part of his household "family" and after his deathwatch over the humble Sotto il Monte museum of his effects. Roncalli esteemed these Sisters of the Poor—he met them also in 1905 while accompanying Radini Tedeschi on a visit— for self-sacrificing lives aiding humanity's weakest.

Among his writings for *La Vita Diocesana* in June 1911, he profiled their founder, Don Luigi Palazzolo (1827–1886), on the twenty-fifth anniversary of his death, "father of orphans, friend of the young, and servant of the poor."[15] Years later, having left Bergamo, letters made clear he never ceased to share the sisters' hopes and dreams for Palazzolo's holiness to be officially recognized by the Church. Who could dream then that he would beatify the man one day?

Roncalli's hallmark obedience led him into political activities with women too. He wrote of himself: "My own natural disposition…indicate[s] calm peaceful work for me, far removed from the field of battle, rather than controversial action, polemics and conflict."[16] But when called by the bishop, he provided leadership to women fighting government efforts to throw voluntary religious instruction out of the area's public schools.

This led to involvement in more social justice and educational groups. As a member and often an officer—even president—of organizations and diocesan commissions, he learned more about committees and about maintaining charity in spite of difficult personalities or anti-Church attitudes.

THE BODY BITES BACK

That his gifts were greatly appreciated was not all blessing. In 1913, for example, Don Angelo was asked to give a ten-lecture series, "The Church, Science and School," for a group called the Popular University for the Catholic Youth Club. Because of the lectures' success, he was asked to give ten more on another topic. In a letter to a priest friend he admitted sometimes feeling overwhelmed by his duties.

From the human point of view, he made the kind of mistakes in this regard to which people trying to love God totally are prone. For one thing, he compared himself with another one of God's friends. On retreat in 1912, while admitting, "Obedience has…overburdened me with so many occupations that my shoulders are sagging under the weight," he noted that "my Bishop…does more than I."[17] And he sought no relief.

On the next retreat, in 1913, he noted that he was tempted (he saw this as a weakness) to ask "to rid myself of some of the burden of my responsibilities and to indicate which of these I would prefer to retain. But I have decided not to do anything about it. My Superiors know everything, and that is enough. As I have not been asked about this, I will be careful not to show my preference for one kind of work rather than another."[18]

With Don Angelo showing no preference nor pointing out his load to them, let alone making even the mildest complaint, the Superiors, probably quite unthinkingly or judging Roncalli's capacity by their own, continued to pile it on. Was this God's design, as Don Roncalli concluded? Or a misunderstanding? Whatever one thinks, this self-sacrifice, prudent or not, became a hallmark of Angelo Roncalli's particular path to holiness.

Already in October 1912, a month before his thirty-second birthday, he noted, "I begin to feel some wear and tear of the nerves." He wrote that this expressed itself in an irritability he tried not to let dominate him to the point that others would see it. He believed his duty as a priest was to "understand and sympathize with everyone, without passing harsh judgments."[19]

Yet stress found an outlet. He wrote, "My miserable body is becoming fat and heavy."[20] Hardly fat at this point, his photos still confirm weight gain. His lifestyle would never again permit those walks all over Rome or other good exercise. And with a healthy appetite—reared without even bread—how could he fail to sit down happily at the full table of even mediocre seminary food or to the modest repast of most rectories?

He had struggled since seminary days against what he then called greediness, although this may have been simply a normal healthy young male's attraction to food. (Archbishop Capovilla years later saw nothing excessive in the amounts Roncalli ate.) At any rate, what the young priest himself regarded as a battle was successful until this point. But during his third decade and onward, struggle as he would, he would keep gaining.

It is a truism that God leaves every saint one or more weaknesses that their most earnest efforts and prayers do not conquer, in order to safeguard them in humility. In the early twenty-first century, when the obese are scorned, thinness almost worshipped, and people suffer the physical, psychological and spiritual illnesses of anorexia and bulimia, God may have decided that adding a fat saint to all the thin ones has merit.

If somewhat wounded in body, nevertheless Angelo Roncalli's spiritual growth in love and in abandonment to Jesus Christ kept pace with his crushing load, enabling him to carry on.

❧ 4 ❧

Drama, Deaths and a
World War I Chaplaincy

ON MAY 22, 1912, AT THE AGE OF EIGHTY-EIGHT, ZAVERIO Roncalli died. His great-nephew, struggling to get there, arrived on May 21 in time to "baptize" by last rites into the greater life the beloved great-uncle who had stood baptismal godfather at his own entry into this world.

A year later Don Roncalli's vibrant bishop began struggling with attacks of terrible intestinal pain. After a year of this, in the spring of 1914, doctors recommended a major remedy of the era, especially for illnesses that could be related to stress: Let the bishop have a change of scene, a greatly reduced schedule and rest. Don Angelo accompanied Radini Tedeschi that May to a villa in Groppino, an area where the bishop wanted to build a vacation residence for Bergamo's seminarians, rather than having them return each summer to their family homes.

Serving as courier on all the bishop's business, Don Roncalli was to and fro between Bergamo and Groppino for the next couple of months. During that time the change of scene did not bring Radini Tedeschi healing. There were respites, but overall a deadly intestinal tumor was gaining ground. Against this painful backdrop the bishop's secretary experienced his first taste of disfavor and attack.

DEFENDING HIMSELF

Four years earlier, in 1910, Don Roncalli had written about (today canonized) Pope Pius X's creation of regional seminaries in central and southern Italy and his reorganization of Roman seminaries, to ensure that what was taught met Pius's criteria for sound ecclesiastical education. In tune with the pope's aims, Angelo wrote:

> Jesus...has shown me in a dazzling light the wisdom, timeliness and nobility of the measures taken by the Pope to safeguard the clergy in particular from the infection of modern errors...,which in a crafty and tempting way are trying to undermine the foundations of Catholic doctrine. The painful experiences of this year...have convinced me...that this wind of Modernism blows very strongly and more widely than seems at first sight.

But Roncalli was unwilling to condemn as deliberately trying to undermine the Church those under fire for offering unsound teaching or books:

[Modernism] may very likely strike and bewilder even those who were at first moved only by the desire to adapt the ancient truth of Christianity to modern needs. Many, some of them good men, have fallen into error, perhaps unconsciously; they have let themselves be swept into [it]. The worst...is that [these] ideas lead very swiftly to the spirit of independence and private judgment about everything and everyone.

In his own seminary teaching, Don Roncalli was and always would be a man of the Church, who looked to her teachings and historical precedents for solutions and wisdom. At the same time he recognized, with Radini Tedeschi, that old truths had to be presented in new ways to reach a new era. It was his skill at imparting to his students staunchness in eternal truths and openness to all else that made his classes the seminary's most popular. He had ended his retreat musings: "I thank the Lord on my knees for having preserved me safely in the midst of such a ferment and agitation of brains and tongues."[1]

But Roncalli became sadly aware that in the Modernist upheaval, Radini Tedeschi was one of the suffering innocent, under the major stress of grief that he, too, had lost the pope's confidence, just at the time he faced great opposition among some of his priests to the summer seminarian residence. To seek support for that project, the very ill bishop sent to Rome the seminary's rector accompanied by charming Don Angelo.

It was with his usual serenity that Don Angelo walked into the office of Cardinal Gaetano De Lai, head of the Congregation for Seminaries. He was not cordially received.

De Lai had heard of Don Roncalli. And what he had heard made him sternly disapproving. In a thorough—and detailed—dressing down, the cardinal classed Bergamo's highly popular Professor Roncalli as one of the so-called Modernists about whom Don Angelo had written four years earlier. Typically, Don Angelo had expressed sympathy for them as probably well-meaning persons.

De Lai gave the priest before him no such credit. Roncalli left dazed and shaken.

He recovered himself praying at the tombs of Saint Peter and Saint Ignatius Loyola.

Then without delay he wrote the cardinal a firm, respectful letter denying every allegation. He maintained, "It seems to me that I have worked with great rectitude and with all my heart, according to my modest strength, by word, pen, and example, in public and private, in the manifold exercise of my priestly ministry, to promote a joyous…love for the Church…and its policies."[2]

De Lai wrote back accepting what was said. But Don Roncalli sent off a second letter in which he—again firmly and charitably—addressed every charge by explaining his teaching in detail, "using concrete and indisputable facts."[3] Finally he offered to take an oath as to the accuracy of all he said. The letter he received back was cordial. Don Angelo had captured De Lai's sword and hammered it into a victor's wreath for himself.

MORE DEATHS

The conflict with De Lai finished in June. Later that month, on June 28, 1914, the assassination of an Austro-Hungarian archduke set off various declarations of war among Europe's nations, culminating in Germany's declaration of war on France that August 3. The Great War, as World War I would be called, had begun. August 4, the eleventh anniversary of Pius X's election, saw the conflict engulfing all Europe. Eventually even Japan and the Ottoman Empire would take up arms in the first *world* conflict.

As millions of men marched out to kill each other, while their women wailed and prayed, some of those sending others to grisly fates wanted the self-justification of receiving Pius X's blessing. "I bless peace, not war," was the saint's attitude.[4] Seventeen days later, after suddenly sickening, he died of a broken heart.

Meanwhile, as the war erupted, Don Roncalli had to shoulder the soul-piercing job of telling Radini Tedeschi he was dying. Leaving the villa entered with such hopes, they returned to Bergamo.

In the midst of all this death, there was a day of joy. On August 14, 1914, the bishop's young secretary took out his journal, celebrating ten years of priesthood—very quietly because "my bishop" lay close at hand so terribly ill. "My dominant thought," he wrote, "in my joy at having accomplished ten years as a priest is this: I do not belong to myself, or to others; I belong to my Lord."[5]

During the same night Pius X was dying in Rome, at three in the morning, not long after having sent Don Roncalli to get some sleep, Radini Tedeschi called him back to his bedside. The weary secretary bent over his dying spiritual father, lovingly reaching out to plump his pillows, and the bishop slumped, weeping loudly, in his spiritual son's arms. In the book he later wrote on Radini Tedeschi, Roncalli reported: "The bishop sobbed like a child.... I said, 'Take courage, bishop. Why are you so troubled? Are we not always in the hands of the Lord, who gives strength and life?' 'Ah, my son,' he replied, 'I am troubled by the thought of my responsibilities. I am a bishop, I am a bishop!'"[6]

But he let Don Angelo convince him that he had not failed God, and calmed, the bishop was able to talk acceptingly of his death, comforting and encouraging the younger man. He spoke words of love and appreciation for all Don Angelo had done for him in their nearly ten years together, words Roncalli described as "the sweetest comforts for my spirit."[7]

With day, visitors started coming and going, making their good-byes, Don Roncalli aiding other staff in attending them as well as—his primary concern—the bishop. At the last, with a few relatives and others making a circle round the bed, he helped Radini Tedeschi focus on God by praying aloud various prayers that the dying man repeated. The biography continues:

> At a certain point, he fell silent and it seemed he was not listening anymore. As soon as he noticed my own silence, he opened his eyes and whispered in my ear, "Courage, courage, Don Angelo. Everything is all right. Do continue. I understand everything, you know." So I continued, "O Jesus Crucified, I willingly offer you the sacrifice of my life, in union with yours on the cross, in atonement for my sins and for the sins of my people, for the Church, the new pontiff, my priests, my seminary,

my country." At this point he opened his eyes and fixed them, it seemed, on a distant vision, then with a strong, clear voice, he added, "And for peace, and for peace."[8]

Minutes later, looking at his secretary-son, the great bishop died "gently, without the slightest spasm," as if falling asleep.[9]

Previously Don Roncalli had recoiled from the ugliness and sadness of death.[10] Now he wrote a friend that the bishop's death suffused his soul with peace, satisfaction and a sad but pure sweetness he could not express. To another he confided that grief over Radini Tedeschi metamorphosed into greater priestly zeal and fervor.[11]

WINDS OF CHANGE

In the loss of his bishop, the death of the pope and the start of war, Don Angelo recognized winds of change for himself. His 1914 retreat notes in his thirty-fourth year speculated on the future.

> I hope they will be years of intense labour, upborne by holy obedience, with a great purpose running through everything, but never a thought straying beyond the bounds of obedience. Preoccupations about the future, which arise from self-love, delay the work of God in us and hinder his purposes, without even furthering our material interests. I need to be very watchful about this,... because I foresee that with the passing of years, and perhaps in the near future, I shall have many struggles with my pride. Let whoever will pass before me and go on ahead; I stay here where Providence has placed me, with no anxieties, leaving the way clear for others.[12]

A new bishop arrived with his own secretary. It was natural that, to Don Angelo, the successor bishop, Luigi Marelli, if a good man, was not of the caliber of "my bishop." Especially he found Marelli lacking in vigor and decisiveness. What was less natural was that the old bishop's secretary's views were written only for himself, not whispered to others. Roncalli did not criticize or undermine Bishop Marelli in any way. Instead he was true to lengthy *Journal* resolutions:

> I shall make a special point of giving my new Bishop...that reverence, obedience and sincere, generous and cheerful affection which, by the grace of God, I was always able to feel for his unforgettable predecessor.... I shall try to set a good example,... [since]in...the Bishop we ought to see...Jesus Christ himself.... May my behaviour give the new Bishop some satisfaction and comfort, so that my person may be not a stumbling block but a block and a tool with which to build.[13]

When he was unsure how to handle something with the new man, he sought Cardinal Ferrari's advice via "a flying visit to Milan...[which] consoled me and cheered me very much."[14] While praying a long time at the tomb of Saint Charles Borromeo in Milan's cathedral, he found the resolution for every sacrifice he might be called to make under the new bishop. Perhaps due to all this, the new bishop thought well of him.

Some were glad to have Radini Tedeschi gone. Don Angelo kept silent again, letting his feelings find an outlet in the memorial book he had begun on the bishop, which ended as both a biography and a collection of the bishop's writings plus statements of praise from others.[15]

On the morning of May 23, 1914, just as he was about to begin Mass for the Feast of Pentecost, someone informed him of his military mobilization. During the Mass he found the grace to abandon himself to God, feeling suddenly even happy to serve in the military as a form of love of neighbor. After Mass he hurried back to the seminary room where he now lived, quickly updated his meager will, ran over to the cathedral to hear Bishop Morelli's homily at another Mass, then dashed to Sotto il Monte to say good-bye to his family.

Early the next day he was in Milan for the call-up, for the second time in his life in military uniform. As a priest he knew he would probably be assigned to the medical corps. Declared "completely fit," he realized that might mean a field hospital at the front. Instead he found himself assigned to his own Bergamo seminary, a newly declared military hospital! Three days after leaving the seminary amid condolences and promises of prayer, he was back in his own room. Ironically, everyone else's had been commandeered to make room for the soldiers.

LIVING TO SERVE

Roncalli's "health sergeant" duties were the menial ones of a medical orderly. He saw to moving the worst-off patients to civilian hospitals; he soaked the endless streams of dirty bedding, bandages and towels in tubs of boiling water and scrubbed them out; he cleaned and disinfected the dormitory he had once slept in—now filled with ill soldiers. On his retreat just after Radini Tedeschi's death, he had worried about being called to occupations where he would struggle with pride. Perhaps he noticed, as he mopped and laundered, that God had taken good care of that.

To the ill and others he gave spiritual comfort where he could, and he organized soldiers' Masses for men stationed in Bergamo. In addition, he enlisted laypeople from Catholic Action to pass out rosaries and religious medals to the troops.

Until all the seminarians were called to war, he kept up some semblance of regular classes for them. He also fit in various endeavors for the Union of Catholic Women and Sunday Masses for the Daughters of the Sacred Heart. He had more chances to get to Sotto il Monte than when he had been a bishop's secretary, and on October 8, 1914, he was at the bedside of his grandfather, Angelo Roncalli, to help the eighty-eight-year-old man leave the world.

Fitting in hospital and field Masses for the troops too, he found himself interacting with Protestants, Muslims and atheists. In an age when scowling Christians of all kinds called down God's wrath on each other, let alone on non-Christians, he decided, "Never mind thunderbolts from heaven! Charity, charity and simple, direct, loving truth!"[16]

His openness extended to ex-Catholics. He wrote, "If they abandon the Church, a large part of the guilt belongs to us priests." Priests, he concluded in a lengthy musing, need to be "holy and apostolic." They need to forgo criticizing the world and humanity, "seize the good wherever we find it...and multiply it." Roncalli's own stance was to see people's souls as "indeed good" and to deal with everyone from "an incorrigibly optimistic outlook. I never met a pessimist" he added, "who accomplished any good."[17]

In 1916 he was promoted to chaplain of a 150-bed military hospital, still in Bergamo. He ministered individually to the patients and to those who tended them, including many sisters, and promoted group spiritual initiatives for the military men. In at least two addresses he gave after the war, he spoke of chaplains' bending "over our dying younger brothers [to] listen to the anguished breathing of the nation [as it was] revealed in their passion and agony."[18]

This phrase was meant to stir listeners' emotions. The reality was simpler and sadder. He wrote in his diary of a nineteen-year-old soldier suffering from bronchial pneumonia, who whispered in Don Roncalli's ear that perhaps it was best that he die now while he felt his soul was still innocent and he would not have to suffer as if he left a wife and children. Deeply moved, Don Roncalli urged the youth to pray for many years of life. The boy rallied but a month later suddenly died. After such deaths, with limbs aching from kneeling at a bedside, the chaplain would return to his room, fall to his knees again and weep.

With such experiences and two of his four brothers at war, one missing in action—he wept for them too—he concluded there was nothing more evil than war. As the nations spurned Pope Benedict XV's peace efforts, on December 5, 1917, Roncalli wrote a soldier brother: "The men who have governed and are governing us do not merit our sacrifices, but the country which today is in peril merits all; men pass but the country remains. In sacrificing ourselves for the nation, we sacrifice ourselves for God and our brothers."[19]

In this spirit of sacrifice, in July 1918 he accepted an optional assignment: moving to a special hospital for ex-prisoners of war suffering from tuberculosis. Always very transmissible, in 1918 TB was widespread, greatly feared and often fatal. "Let God's will be done," he wrote in his diary. "I do this work of charity willingly, offering my life in sacrifice to the Lord, to atone for my sins and negligence, and for the good of the Church and of my brethren."[20]

To a friend he wrote good-humoredly, "I will likely enjoy the reward for simplicity and remain untouched."[21] Which he did. Tucked away in the germ-filled TB hospital, he was less exposed to the even more deadly 1918 flu pandemic, which killed millions, including his twenty-five-year-old youngest sister.

Because so many of these broken young TB patients were dying panting for breath—the image he later used for the nation in postwar talks—he expected to die soon too.

As 1918 and the war ended, Chaplain Roncalli was offered a governmental honor for his sacrificial work. He turned it down. Nothing he had done had been for the government.

❧ 5 ❧

Teacher and Guide

FOR ONE EXPECTING TO DIE, ANGELO RONCALLI'S DESTINY took a very lively turn. Bishop Marelli had entrusted him that February with bringing to life a revolutionary idea, a *Casa degli studenti* ("house of students"). There young Catholic laymen could live and gather to strengthen their faith while pursuing higher education in institutions that often put that faith to the test.

In April 1919, on retreat, Roncalli noted that this apostolate to students was definitely God's choice for him and vowed: "I shall love my young students as a mother her sons."[1] He recorded desires to bring them up apostles of truth and goodness and worthy sons of the Church.

Happily the chosen site was so close to the seminary that Don Roncalli could readily run between his lively students and the seminarians returning from war.

For the first time he had living quarters he had to furnish. Helped by a modest gift from his father, Don Roncalli discovered the aesthetic pleasures of what one could call "design" and "decorating" if his situation had not been so modest. But he would never become an aesthete. He wrote on that spring 1919 retreat:

> It is now some months since I set up my own home and furnished it in a suitable manner. Nevertheless, perhaps now more than ever before, the Lord gives me to understand the beauty and the sweetness of the spirit of poverty. I feel I would be willing to give it all up here and now, and without regrets. I shall always try, as long as I live, to keep this feeling of detachment from all that is mine.[2]

Up to November of 1919 under his bishop, Don Roncalli was also again hard at work on behalf of young women. Beginning in 1918 he made a number of trips to Milan, aiding those giving birth to the Association for Young Catholic Women. Then he passed long hours over many months finding the right women for the first local groups.

He worked with another bishop to start a newsletter for the women. Its topics included the social and political, such as education, problems of workers and divorce, as well as specifically religious ones plus Catholic social doctrine.

In November 1919 there was a conference with three important speakers—one actually a woman—to officially inaugurate the movement in the diocese. In his diary Don Angelo recorded his joy at the success of the conference and of the new organization after "my work of silent and almost hidden preparation."[3] Because of the promise he saw in the new organization, he ended his decade of endeavors for women "content."

A LOAD FOR HIS SHOULDERS

After fifteen years as a priest, Roncalli's role appeared fixed as an educator of the minds and souls of young people—a well-liked, able seminary professor, a highly regarded teacher of local women in formation for religious orders, a popular teacher of young laity and a path-breaking student residence director.

His remaining diocesan tasks were a good fit: those independent historical researches (he was asked to do a new commemorative work and talk for the start of the 1919 academic year), publications and association with various diocesan periodicals. It seemed his career was set in his Bergamo diocese. His status was more modest than some of his early dreams, but he accepted it as God's will for him and was happy.

Then came a new assignment. Uncharacteristically, he tried to get out of it, feeling real uncertainty that he was at the spiritual level the job needed. Failing to be let off, in summer 1919, relying on God's help, he shouldered the heavy burden of being spiritual director to the Bergamo seminarians.

In order to have the time to work with each seminarian one on one, he was relieved of all his other responsibilities except directing the House of Studies. No task of his had ever received this consideration. But no task is more vital to the Church, as Don Roncalli knew from his own experience, than the formation that readies a man to become a good, even holy, priest.

Forming the older seminarians of 1919 was an especially difficult task. Those who survived their war service to return—fourteen from Bergamo's seminary were dead—were not the innocent seminarians of Don Roncalli's youth. They had seen up close as much, maybe more, suffering and death than he, without his maturity. Some bore jagged spiritual and psychological wounds.

Don Angelo relied on the charism called "the discernment of spirits"[4] to help each seminarian with his weekly confession, personal spiritual direction (when requested), monthly retreat and various community and individual spiritual exercises. Only too aware that what he *was* spoke more loudly than what he advised, he did his best, with God's help, to offer each young man the same good example and fatherly love he had received from his own spiritual guides.

While he officially had no other tasks, because of his organizational skills (which he denied), coupled with a temperament that almost anyone could get along with, he was a planner for the September 1920 Sixth Eucharistic Congress, held right in Bergamo. He was scheduled to introduce speakers at the congress, not to speak. But when the bishop slated to give the opening address canceled at the last minute, Don Roncalli was tapped to replace him with only the night before to prepare.

His speech blended the traditional elements of eucharistic devotion and devotion to Jesus' mother with frank talk about the moment's postwar social and political unrest. The people seated before him were afraid of a possible Communist revolution, such as the one in full eruption in Russia. Don Roncalli assured them that their faith was equal to finding gospel-based solutions to every problem Italian society faced. The stand-in speaker received a standing ovation.

Thus Don Roncalli's name was spread somewhat beyond the diocese. He was invited to "say a few words" to a roomful of cardinals and bishops while visiting his old Roman seminary. And a cardinal in Bologna had him give spiritual exercises to a group of his laity.

OF WIDE-RANGING SYMPATHIES

While Roncalli would always remain utterly obedient to the Church's hierarchy and policies, his wide-ranging sympathies sometimes led him to insights beyond those of his contemporaries in the Church and without. For instance, during the war he had written in his private notes of the mealtime discussions among his seminary colleagues critical of his initiatives for the soldiers: "These excellent and upright priests live...among their books... see[ing] the war only from a distance. Although good,... they are completely ignorant of real life."[5]

Peasant-born Roncalli understood that Italy's farmers and workers had new aspirations. He also understood all those—particularly the middle-class people who had no understanding of peasant farmers' or workers' lives—who clung to Italy's tradition of hierarchical society, where someone "above me" has my loyalty and must in turn protect me. These elements in the Church and society wanted to apply this paternalism to workers in the new factories. Don Roncalli knew firsthand both the good and the insufficiency of paternalism. It was one of the Roncallis' landlords, a priest, who had paid much of Angelo Roncalli's seminary fees. Under the same landlords he also gained personal experience of poverty so extreme that children shivered indoors in winter while mothers and fathers, in spite of their backbreaking labor, could only shiver with them.

As factories became bigger, the more benign—at least in theory—paternalism gave way to owners' viewing workers *en masse*, impersonally. Employers looked for ways to keep labor cheap and to make revolt illegal. Roncalli knew, as the 1920s opened, that labor *was* uniting—even though many areas had laws against this—and that the Church needed to be with the people, lest she leave the workers to the warped compassion and illusory brotherhood of Communism or to sins of hatred and violence. He remembered, if others had forgotten, Leo XIII's *Rerum Novarum,* the encyclical that positioned the Church as with, not against, its workers, without ceasing also to shepherd employers.

So Don Roncalli supported the Labor Office arm of Catholic Action. Unfortunately, radical elements among the clergy and laity got power there and tried to turn labor to an aggressive, adversarial approach. This in turn led to attacks on the Labor Office by many in the Church. With his acquired wisdom and innate balance of temperament, Don Roncalli was not swept up in the conflict. His stand, whether others could see it or not, would always be the teachings of Jesus Christ as proclaimed by the Church.

Over half a century earlier, in 1860, the papal states had been invaded and wrested—ultimately beneficially—from the Church. Pius IX had picked up the political marbles for all Italy's Catholics and said, "We won't play anymore." Good Catholics reluctantly left politics.

Sixty years later, post–World War I Catholics, both inside Catholic Action and outside it, realized they had to participate fully in politics or prepare for far worse losses. A new national postwar political party, calling itself the Popular

Party, formed. The Popular Party had Catholic ideals but a nonsectarian platform open to alliances with all of goodwill. In an age of great religious intolerance in all Christianity, this led to suspicion by some in the Church.

Don Roncalli noted the predilection of certain clergy and Church groups to criticize and tear down what Catholic Action or other Catholic groups tried to do to create a more Christian society. This, he noted in his diary in February 1919, gave "our enemies reason to laugh at us and work for our destruction."[6]

In spite of all the local suspicion, Don Roncalli saw that the new party caught the aspirations of many Catholics and would succeed. As he predicted, it won a landslide victory in the area that November. His diary notes: "We are always taking new steps forward toward the re-vindication of the Christian spirit in the public arena. That is a great good for which we must thank the Lord."[7]

"WHERE GOD CALLS"

When he was tapped to be bishop of Bergamo in 1905, Professor Radini Tedeschi was working in the papal secretariat of state with another monsignor named Giacomo Della Chiesa. At the banquet following Radini Tedeschi's elevation to bishop, Monsignor Della Chiesa and the bishop-elect's new secretary, Don Roncalli, enjoyed a friendly conversation. Four years later Bishop Radini Tedeschi took Don Angelo along when he spent a week or so visiting his friend Giacomo, by then the archbishop of Bologna.

Della Chiesa was elected pope, becoming Benedict XV, on September 3, 1914, just after Radini Tedeschi's and Pius X's deaths. He had barely been named a cardinal in time for the conclave. The new pope graciously wrote a foreword for young Roncalli's book on Radini Tedeschi, and Roncalli dedicated the book to him.

In 1921 Benedict XV was handed a list of possible priests to head a new central office that would promote and reorganize the efforts of Italy's dioceses to support the Vatican congregation for the Church's missions throughout the world, a work dear to Benedict's heart. It is said the pope ran his eyes down the list and exclaimed with excitement, "This one. This one!" He was pointing to the name Don Angelo Roncalli. And that is how the well-settled Bergamo apostle of youth was invited to become a monsignor in Rome and the new council president in charge of revitalizing this work in Italy under the direction of a Vatican cardinal.[8]

After working so hard to give up all ecclesiastical ambition, Don Roncalli hesitated, full of scruples. Was this truly God's will for him? To preclude the slightest self-seeking, he presented Bishop Marelli with a list of his *non*-qualifications for the job. And he contacted a peer in Milan, secretary to Cardinal Ferrari, and asked if his friend could try to see what the cardinal thought. The cardinal, who had lost his voice to throat cancer and would be dead in six weeks, wrote Don Roncalli: "God's will is more than manifest. Where God calls one goes, without hesitation, abandoning himself to the Lord's loving Providence."[9]

And so, with Don Roncalli's always tender heart "bleeding" at separation from "all that I love so much,"[10] he left his seminarians, his house of students and his lifelong Bergamo roots and moved to Rome.

❧ 6 ❧

At Home in Rome

RONCALLI REJOICED TO PUT HIMSELF AT ONCE UNDER THE spiritual direction of his old Roman seminary spiritual director, Father Francesco Pitocchi, with whom he had kept in touch through letters and counsel-seeking visits. Pitocchi would remain his director for two years until the holy Redemptorist's death on June 13, 1922.

Roncalli had two unmarried sisters whom he brought from Sotto il Monte to keep house for him. As soon as the trio could move to slightly larger quarters, he offered a home to his aged former Roman seminary rector, Monsignor Vincenzo Bugarini, an "amiable, simple, pious man—always serene and smiling."[1]

At the missions office things ran smoothly. Those who worked there benefited from Roncalli's sweet, accepting nature and, if they did not already share it, soon entered into his zeal for reorganizing Italian efforts to better spread the faith in far-off lands. Even when lights burned late there was cheerful camaraderie.

Vocations—which were plentiful—and financial help for the missions were part of postwar renewal and spirituality among the devout. The missionary congregation had its own seminary in Rome and a residence at Castel Gondolfo where its seminarians vacationed. In June 1923 Roncalli invited the Sisters of the Poor to Rome. Ten sisters happily split charge of the kitchens and wardrobe at the two institutions.

By Benedict XV's decree, published just four days before he died, on January 22, 1922, at the exact hour he had foretold, Monsignor Roncalli had become more than the president of the central council for Italy. From Rome under the same cardinal, while continuing his Italian responsibilities, he now was also heading the Church's central office. Newly moved from Lyon, France, the central office was the place to which those in posts comparable to his in Europe's other countries reported.

His most time-consuming job remained encouraging and directing donations for the missions from all over Italy and, to that end, maintaining rapport with Italy's local diocesan missions directors and their bishops. What helped was the fact that he frequently came through their doors with warm messages from Monsignor Bugarini, who had shepherded many of these men toward the priesthood. Italian mission donations more than doubled.

As always in life, there were flies in the ointment. Roncalli came to understand that sweetness and light were not the usual case in Vatican offices. His rapport with his staff caused envy in some. Moreover, those putting out missionary magazines saw his new bulletin as competition. Trying cheerfully and gently to draw everyone's efforts together for the great cause, if he generally succeeded it was because he was willing to give lavish credit to others' work and minimize his own.

Turning forty on November 25, 1921, Roncalli had a premonition that this would be his final year of life. This was not because his energy or vitality were flagging. However, he had developed his first medical problem. From giving many speeches in his travels, his voice had given way severely. Doctors treated him for a month and ordered another month of absolute silence.

Among his friends was the sister of his beloved Radini Tedeschi, Mother Maria Felice, superior of the Ursuline Sisters of Piacenza. At her invitation he passed September 6 through October 4, 1921, with their community in Rapallo. Dutifully practicing silence there, he wrote Monsignor Bugarini, "I still do not have the courage to ask [God] to give me back my voice." And he added in the same letter to his old rector that he felt only joy to leave it to God's "pleasure and wish." The voice returned.[2]

EVERYBODY'S FAVORITE MONSIGNOR

In Rome Monsignor Roncalli's priestly dedication and personal qualities made him the monsignor everyone loved. Consequently he was invited to just about every parish and confraternity to speak.

Here too religious sisters were fans. His feet were barely on Roman pavement in 1921 when he became chaplain to the city's Sisters of the Cenacle. For their students he gave a course on religion similar to those he had presented to groups in Bergamo. In November he accepted the position of chaplain for the Daughters of Mary, giving retreats and teachings for them each year.

He did not cut ties with Bergamo's sisters either. He had started helping two groups get their rules recognized, one in 1918, the other in 1920. He continued to work on their behalf until the second won approval in 1922 and the first, after ten arduous years, in 1928. And he did not forget his Bergamo collaborators for youth, the Daughters of the Sacred Heart. He was soon a friend of their Rome community on Via Cavour. That house, the one in Milan and later one in Venice would always be his "hotels."

After three years in Rome, he happily revisited being an educator, assigned to teach a course in patrology at the Lateran Seminary. The cream of the Church's seminarians acclaimed each of Monsignor Roncalli's lectures with applause. Ever more interiorly concentrated on union with God and indifference to the plaudits or censure of humankind, Don Roncalli was equal to all this esteem.

As Roncalli dashed about, Monsignor Bugarini tended the home fires like a good papa. Then a sudden bronchial pneumonia carried the amiable old rector away on February 14, 1924, Angelo and his sisters at his side. Shortly after the death Roncalli wrote home how much he missed Monsignor Bugarini's smile.

The aged priest left his friend the chalice given him on his ordination and his typewriter. Once Monsignor Roncalli got the hang of it, he sent no more handwritten letters.

NEW PERILS, NEW FRIEND

Since 1922 the Fascists—born as an elite military fighting unit during the war—were in power. Their leader, Benito Mussolini, had become premier through a show of force before a paralyzed government. Fascism used violence and intimidation to cow voters and those in the government and the press who might fight them. An anti-Church atheist, Mussolini made a show of accommodation with the Church, putting crucifixes back in Italy's classrooms. However, this was done *only* for the elementary grades. The Fascist leader's plans for the older students he aimed to recruit were not compatible with Christ.

Roncalli was not fooled. In 1924 he planned to vote for the anti-Fascist Popular Party but ended up not voting at all. In his position he was not supposed to take sides, and apparently his vote would not have remained secret. Although Christians and other anti-Fascists won a number of seats in Parliament, soon non-Fascist political figures and opinion makers scurried into hiding or exile before they could be imprisoned or murdered.

Through his involvement with students, Monsignor Roncalli had a new friend, a younger prelate from the Secretariat of State named Giovanni Battista Montini, one day to become Pope Paul VI. Montini's father was both a Popular Party member of the government as well as a leading newspaper publisher. The elder Montini would have his newspaper closed and stop attending Parliament sessions after the Fascists kidnapped and murdered a colleague.

In this atmosphere, in September 1924 a Mass commemorated Radini Tedeschi in Bergamo, and Monsignor Roncalli

gave the homily. Many local dignitaries and government officials were present when Roncalli spoke lovingly of Radini
Tedeschi, then segued to the dead bishop's political attitudes
to deliver a firm statement against Fascism. Afterward
Monsignor Roncalli and Bishop Marelli waited to see what
the result would be for Roncalli. Perhaps *this* Bergamo priest's
ecclesiastical rise was over.

The pope succeeding Benedict XV, Achille Ratti, Pius
XI, was the former head of Milan's Ambrosian Library. It was
he who had helped Roncalli with his research on Saint
Charles Borromeo when Roncalli was Radini Tedeschi's secretary. Ratti had abandoned the Popular Party for fear they
would seek alliances leftward. Fascism played on fears of
Communism: Mussolini stretched out his hand opportunisti-
cally to the Church, and the frightened Pius took it.

Yet the waters remained calm around Roncalli, with just
one strange ripple: an unjustified attack on his preparations
for the 1925 Holy Year by the cardinal under whom he
worked. Someone was bad-mouthing Roncalli. Equal to
esteem, he was also equal to its opposite. He wrote in his diary
that he looked only to God for "satisfaction and rewards."[3]

He found both in his work. He felt blessed at being part
of what many considered a new Pentecost, in which the Holy
Spirit was again inspiring zealous souls to carry the faith to
the ends of the earth and inspiring those who stayed home to
sacrifice their children and treasure to this high purpose.

OF HOLY JOY AND HUMAN SORROW

Awash in efforts to personally evangelize locally and to promote and financially support worldwide evangelization,

Roncalli was chided for working too hard. Yet like a latter-day Saint Paul, the love of Christ urged him on (see 2 Corinthians 5:14). He branded himself, in his January 1924 retreat notes, as someone he should always humbly think of as "a lazy fellow, a beast of burden that ought to do much more work and get on with it much faster."[4]

It is clear that at some level he knew this was not true. Few priests were carrying his workload. His words reflected the spiritual frustration that, do what he would, his human capacity would never equal his desire to see every soul as blessed as he who could honestly journal regarding his work, "The Lord gives me indescribable happiness."[5] He also wrote, a bit too optimistically, that here he would stay without a thought or glance backward toward his Bergamo seminarians or hostel.

Another twelve months and his life took a new, sharp-angle turn: He was made a bishop, an archbishop even, but—to his family he dubbed it the thorn in the rose—he was being sent to Bulgaria. He was banished, in effect, from Rome and his great success there, into ecclesiastical exile.

Bulgaria in 1925 was strongly anti-Catholic. A Catholic bishop would not be allowed to preach to or teach the vast majority of Bulgaria's Christians, Orthodox who would shun him like the plague. Roncalli's pastoral heart would find only the tiniest handful of Bulgarian—and resident foreign—Catholics to shepherd.

Someone had done him dirt. Roncalli took it with scarcely a murmur, his letter home trying to encourage his family, sad to see him go so far away, that, thorn or not, his being named a bishop was an unsought honor for them and the parish. He intended to be, he concluded, a bishop who cared only for saving and sanctifying souls.

An audience with Pius XI increased his peace. For him the will of the pope was the will of God. But that did not keep him from weeping alone in his room.[6]

The middle-aged sisters, who had dedicated their lives to him and for whom this was a terrible blow, cried too. They returned to Sotto il Monte, never to live with their beloved Angelo again.

During a preparatory retreat he wrote, "'It is the duty of bishops,' says St. Thomas, 'to be perfect and teachers of perfection.' This is a terrifying thought for me, for I feel and know myself to be very helpless and incapable! Another reason for remaining humble, very, very humble!"[7]

He also wrote about the bishop's motto he selected:

"I insert in my coat of arms the words *Obedientia et Pax* (Obedience and Peace) which [Cardinal] Cesare Baronius used to say every day, when he kissed the Apostle's [statue's] foot in St Peter's. These words are in a way my own history and my life." Then follows an oddly prophetic sentence: "O may there be the glorification of my humble name through the centuries!"[8]

Roncalli was consecrated archbishop March 19, 1925. Some of his family were awed to attend the first Mass their bishop said—once again at Saint Peter's tomb—and meet the pope. The new archbishop's own eyes saw only a Way of the Cross in the honor that ended his happy life of loved work and companionship, especially with his sisters. Clinging to God's help, he boarded a train to Bulgaria.

❧ 7 ❧

Bulgarian Exile

THE WELCOME WAS MEAGER WHEN ARCHBISHOP RONCALLI stepped down from his two day trip onto a platform in Sofia's train station. Neither civil authorities nor Orthodox representatives greeted the pope's apostolic visitor. But two figures in black proved to be Catholic clergy. One was standing in for the Byzantine bishop, whose seat was vacant. The duo were Archbishop Roncalli's sole escorts to a tiny residence on Rue Liouline.

In this nonecumenical age, when the Orthodox press *did* note Roncalli's arrival, it was to see him as a representative of "Latin imperialism," in Bulgaria for such nefarious purposes as proselytizing innocent Orthodox. In his fatherly style Roncalli set out to do all he could to soften such fears and "make... [the pope] loved."[1]

Two weeks before his arrival—nearly seven years after Russia's Communists successfully killed *their* king—Bulgaria's

Communists had tried to assassinate King Boris III. They set off a bomb in a crowded church where Boris was taking part in a state funeral for a Communist-assassinated government figure. There were many casualties, but the king escaped unhurt. With many still hospitalized, Roncalli immediately obtained the king's permission to visit these wounded. No stranger to the grisly, the former wartime chaplain headed for the hospital. Full of genuine desire to console and comfort, he visited bed to bed.

TENDING THE FLOCK

In spite of its mountains, 1925 Bulgaria was a country where almost everyone worked the land. A month after his arrival, in May, then again in June, Roncalli went into the hinterlands to meet the pope's flock, searching them out in rough carts, on horseback or mule back. A son of poverty himself, he was not put off entering wretched homes of mud bricks. Soon the grapevine preceded him: a true father full of warmth and compassion was coming. Sometimes riding a mule, he entered villages to flocks of running children or lines of villagers on either side of the road welcoming him. He gave and received much love.

But how he wished he had something concrete to give too! He dreamed of bringing those impoverished children the priests and nuns of the Salesian Order with their vocational schools. And for solitary priests so abjectly poor they had to farm just to survive, at the very least, he wrote Rome, there should be oil to light the lamps in their pitiful little chapels. Almost nothing of what he wanted to do to relieve poverty and discouragement, he found, could he do.

At least for the Eastern rite Catholics, twenty months after his arrival, in December 1926, he was able to fill their bishop's chair. He prayed that the new Byzantine rite bishop would get some hearing in Rome, where he knew there was only so much money for the missions, and sadly, almost every other place promised better "return" in souls than thinly scattered Catholics in Bulgaria's solidly Orthodox expanse.

Roncalli had been told he'd be in Bulgaria just long enough to report on the needs of the nation's Catholics and to accomplish four missions: (1) find candidates for that bishop's chair, (2) locate and regroup Eastern rite Catholics, unwelcome war refugees from places like Turkey and Macedonia, (3) stabilize a new Bulgarian congregation, the Eucharistine Sisters, and (4) establish seminaries for training Bulgaria's clergy in country instead of out, a situation that played on Orthodox fears of foreign influences and Roman imperialism.

After this skim-milk posting was to come the cream: service in thoroughly Catholic Brazil, then a return to Rome for actual training as a diplomat.

But Rome's plans changed. Roncalli's Bulgarian exile would last ten difficult years.

SOME SUCCESSES

Third of the four goals was to develop the new order of nuns. Using funds from Rome, one way he did this was by buying land and building them a novitiate, an orphanage and a social services center.

Another way he aided the sisters' development was by engaging them in the second goal: regrouping Catholic refugees pouring into Bulgaria, who were only too often persecuted—even murdered—by Bulgarians suspicious of their politics. His mandate included building and staffing churches for these refugees when possible, as well as— more pressing—keeping them alive. With a hundred thousand lire the Holy Father gave him in January 1926, he set up a kitchen run by the Eucharistines to feed 250 of the poorest refugee children in a remote area two days out of Sofia. A second kitchen elsewhere provided other children with a life-saving daily meal. He wrote home poignantly of the plight of these persecuted peoples, especially the oldest and youngest, in their war-induced misery.

Sometimes with the highest motives, the Vatican stonewalled other worthy initiatives. At times the reasons were as simple as three Vatican Congregations' having jurisdiction over the same work and being unable to agree among themselves. Whatever the various causes, the results for Roncalli were frequent, intense frustration, particularly in regard to his fourth mandate: building minor and major seminaries.

Following many painfully trying delays, in 1929 he received the go-ahead to buy land for the seminary. In the name of the Holy See, a large down payment was made and a contract signed. This happy day was not followed by construction but by more dithering and vacillating in Rome.

On Rome's say-so, in the face of these interminable delays, Roncalli time and again assured complaining Bulgarians to just be patient. Suddenly one day he was instructed to get the former landowners to void the signed contract. Plans had changed. No seminary would be built. The chagrined apostolic visitor lost *his* patience.

Those in the know said someone had been whispering in Pope Pius XI's ear against Roncalli. On the other hand, it is said that later Pius XI smilingly called Roncalli's outburst "the ire of the lamb." Still, the Vatican's reply was blistering and accusatory: The pope's delegate had acted improperly, not waiting for directions.

Monsignor Roncalli refused to let his strong feelings stop his spiritual ascent. He humbled himself before the undeserved lash, writing in private notes that the embarrassment and the blistering would aid humility and help him seek God alone. Hard as it was, he would leave in God's hands what prospered and what failed, choosing charity, forgiveness and humility over any work, however important or worthy.

A Way of the Cross

As Roncalli's fiftieth birthday passed in November 1930, he reflected:

> I…deem it characteristic for true servants of the Lord to feel themselves called to do one thing and instead to have to do another. In a way, that is what is happening [to me].… I have an unmerited office of honor and the power to govern, which I cannot even exercise as [much as] a simple priest does. Rarely do I have an occasion to give a spiritual talk, and I never hear confessions. Often I spend the whole day in front of the typewriter [sending at least twenty detailed reports to Rome on the needs of Bulgaria's impoverished, conflicted Latin and Eastern rites—tiring, tedious work that generally vanished into a bureaucratic abyss] or [I'm] engaged in annoying conversations, discussing difficulties and

problems with people who, while belonging to Jesus Christ and by right to the Catholic Church, have little sensus Christi [Christian sense] and even less sensus Ecclesiae [ecclesial sense]. I am always in contact with so-called important people who are narrow-minded regarding spiritual things. I carefully prepare for events from which I expect a very good outcome and then I see the frailty of human hope.[2]

To Gustavo Testa he confided in an understatement that it did not make a good impression on the Bulgarians when Rome's man seemed to do nothing.

But perhaps those who thwarted Roncalli were not wholly without wisdom. The fact that the Church's shrinking building funds bypassed Bulgaria in the years of worldwide economic depression after October 1929 could be called providential: for the Salesian vocational schools, the minor and major seminaries, the Benedictine center for culture and the arts and other good institutions Roncalli dreamed of for his Bulgarians would have been confiscated by the Communists little more than a decade after he left Bulgaria, and those running them likely murdered.

The real fruit—the most lasting, anyway—of his work in Bulgaria was in his own soul. In a letter to Mother Maria Felice Radini Tedeschi, he confided he'd had one of those transforming graces in which the mystical meaning of events is glimpsed. He described "my life here at Sofia: to work always and secretly, to work at things that aren't seen and are apparently of no importance but which undoubtedly are preparing a good future for the holy Church." He told this spiritual friend that he couldn't thank God enough for calling him to this work, insisting, "I am sincere." If he should end up dead in a ditch somewhere in the Bulgarian hinterlands, he believed even that would "be useful for me and for...souls."[3]

On September 26, 1931, Roncalli was named Bulgaria's first apostolic *delegate* in fifty years, an honor that changed nothing. Roncalli never gave up hope but now serenely accepted, as one of the stations on his Bulgarian Way of the Cross, that no seminary would be built. Many other worthy initiatives he laid out for the Church in Bulgaria and for Catholic-Orthodox reconciliation also withered and died.

But through it all, remaining in the new spiritual dimension, he could say, "I almost no longer know where I left my own will. Now it is somewhat like an amputated leg...no longer there, thanks be to God, but occasionally...mak[ing] itself felt."[4]

THE DIPLOMACY OF THE SAINTS
Never sent for diplomatic training, Roncalli chose the diplomacy of the saints – simple, loving, genuine pastoring outreach. Always acting in the name of the pope, not his own, he attempted, one person or group at a time, to open Orthodox minds and hearts to their Western Christian brothers. "Catholics and Orthodox," he wrote, "are not enemies, but brothers."[5]

As early as 1927 he managed to meet some Orthodox leaders. By bringing Christian love, not polemics, to these skittish fellow Christians, he softened their fears and discovered that both the head of the Bulgarian Orthodox Christians and the patriarch of Constantinople, whom he met on a trip to Turkey, dreamed of unity as he did.

Opening the minds of his foreign Catholic flock to the Bulgarians among whom they lived was harder. No dreams of unity there. Most huddled in tight national groups spiritually and culturally. Most did not try to learn Bulgarian and utterly rejected Roncalli's desire to use a little bit of it at church so that Bulgarians might feel welcome.

Roncalli could only sigh and himself study the language, every other bedtime setting aside his Latin Bible to read the Scriptures in Bulgarian.

Catholics in Bulgaria, he found, didn't get along with each other either. Besides rivalries within the Latin rite, Latin rite Catholics generally looked down on the less numerous Eastern rite Catholics.

Not that uncommon were incidents like the one in which a hundred Thracians and three hundred Macedonians—all Catholics—became very "heated" when talking to the papal representative about each other. He listened to all sides with patience but inner distress. To bring them together, in 1927 he started inviting all the Catholic priests of Sofia for a meal on each anniversary of his episcopal consecration, which was also the feast of Saint Joseph. He believed that in such "a country of dis-union," anything aimed "to correct and cure such a great evil is particularly blessed by the Lord."[6]

THE EARTHQUAKE

In April 1928 Roncalli had a chance to demonstrate Christian brotherhood to the Orthodox and be a father to many, whatever their faith. A large, destructive earthquake struck, its epicenter in Plovdiv, a city in Bulgaria's center that happened to be home to many Eastern rite Catholics.

Roncalli rushed to cold, rain-drenched Plovdiv, where frightening and destructive aftershocks forced him into the muddy streets with everyone else.

He appealed immediately to Pius XI, who responded with half a million lire. Roncalli's home diocese of Bergamo also sent money. Roncalli was happy to report that Catholic help was the first to arrive in Plovdiv, a fact that was widely noticed in the Orthodox nation.

As always, every Roncallian charity was done in the name of the pope, with the thought of making the Church and its vicar loved. But the one who became loved in Bulgaria was the man who, at risk of his own life, disinterestedly used the pope's donation to do Bulgarians good.

In 1929, a year after the earthquake, Roncalli celebrated his twenty-fifth anniversary of priestly ordination. His reaction to the festivities showed that his willingness to walk the Way of the Cross did not preclude enjoyment of life's Palm Sundays. He wrote home—characteristically, toward the end of a long letter about other matters:

> ... grand solemnities in Sofia with two bishops and many representatives from all over Bulgaria. Everybody exerted themselves to do honor [consciously or no, he leaves out the "to me"]: speeches, telegrams, letters, gifts of things from the countryside without end. Gifts that were precious because they were all handmade.... [The Bulgarians]...had insisted on showing me that under their rather rude hides, they have good hearts. And this has given me great comfort, because it lets me

understand that when one works with a right intention
and for the glory of God, the fruits…are not lacking.[7]

OF POPES AND RULERS AND THOSE WHO GO BETWEEN

Still wooing the Church, that same year Fascist leader
Mussolini fathered the Lateran treaty, which restored relations severed in 1871 between Italy and the Vatican state.
Roncalli applauded Mussolini for doing what intervening
governments had not. Those who sixty years later saw this as
pro-Fascism did not understand that Roncalli's poor opinion
of Mussolini would not prevent his recognizing something
good done by the man.

Bulgaria had only been a nation with particular bound-
aries and a kingly dynasty since 1908. Boris III actually had
Catholic family origins. The king and the pope's man got
along well and met many times, with only positive feelings on
both sides, especially since Roncalli did not try to convert any
Orthodox, as had been feared he might.

When the Orthodox king wished to marry the Catholic
daughter of Italy's king and queen, Roncalli helped in very
delicate and protracted negotiations with the pope. Finally, in
a 1930 Catholic ceremony in Assisi, Boris wed Princess
Giovanna of Savoy. Pius XI had given permission based on
Boris's signing the paper required in that era for mixed mar-
riages, promising that children would be raised Catholic. Pius
had also extracted a promise that only the Catholic marriage
would occur.

Boris, however, was an Orthodox king of an Orthodox
people, his rule menaced by forces outside as well as inside
Bulgaria. He absolutely had to avoid angering the Orthodox

Church or the people he ruled. So once in Bulgaria, the couple immediately had an Orthodox wedding. The pope was angry and would be angrier still a few years later when Boris's daughter and son were baptized Orthodox, a requirement if the boy were to reign in Bulgaria.

Boris invited papal representative Roncalli and the country's Catholic bishops to the Orthodox wedding reception. Not only did none attend, Pius XI expected Archbishop Roncalli to send Boris a stiff letter scolding his dishonorable behavior. As Roncalli on many occasions said of himself, his was a nature to understand, not to scold. But he did what he had to do, not with outrage but with wise prudence. He took no credit, amazed, he said, that the Lord helped him "carry out... [this] duty... with great charity and tact before the powerful of the world in order to preserve good relations and not burn any bridges for the future."[8]

How well he succeeded cannot be measured by the official Bulgarian response: He was banned from royal functions for a year, and angry Orthodox demanded he be thrown out of the country. A truer measure is the great esteem both king and queen always had for Roncalli personally, the queen often slipping in to attend the archbishop's Mass. If Roncalli understood Boris's position, Boris understood Roncalli's as well.

Before the archbishop left the country years later, Boris—having honored him with the nation's highest decoration—said to Giovanna in front of Roncalli, for whom they were having a farewell dinner, "What shall we offer the bishop who is leaving us? We will give him this cross [a sixteenth-century piece] so closely linked to our marriage that became for him the cause of such pain."

As for Giovanna, she was such an admirer of Roncalli that she told him she was sure he would be pope one day. "We'll come and visit you in the Vatican," she promised with a smile.[9] She and her children did but, sadly, without Boris. Crushed between the Nazi menace and the Communist one, he was dead.

LONELINESS

As the years passed, another silent suffering was loneliness. Roncalli's appeals for bigger quarters with room for his sisters came to nothing. Raised in a vital home of many happy people, he was stuck in a tiny residence with an aged Bulgarian priest secretary—no kindred spirit—who teetered between death and ill health but had secret stores of energy for perpetual warfare with the also old, shrewish housekeeper. For a man used to households living in Christian charity, the atmosphere was painful.

Roncalli practiced patience. When he finally told the woman that he had to replace her with Eucharistine sisters due to her disrespect for the now crippled old priest, the unrepentant housekeeper served for the next meal—nothing.[10]

Rumors that Roncalli could be moved to a better posting in Budapest ended with someone else chosen. He had done nothing to further his cause, nor had he the previous year during stronger rumors of his being named to Milan. His attitude: "I neither desire to stay nor leave this post. I'm here by obedience and here I wish to stay until [it] pleases the Holy Father without getting in a lather or thinking of other [posts]."[11]

His lack of unhealthy ego did not diminish the pain of his loneliness. But he chose to respond to suffering by making it a prayer offering, turning it into something redemptive for himself and others. "I kiss my cross and thank the Lord who has found me worthy to carry it for the good of souls and of the Church that I wish to serve living or dying."[12] By such responses, at some point in Bulgaria Roncalli crossed the threshold of holiness.

In another creative response, he softened his many months of isolation each year with a steady stream of letters to friends. These included companions from his seminary days; close clerical friends from Bergamo; laypeople in the Bergamo-Milan axis with whom he had collaborated; various mother superiors from orders he had befriended and for whom he still did favors, such as helping the Little Sisters of the Poor with the cause of their founder; friends made in Rome or in his travels all over Italy for the Propaganda; and churchmen met during new travels near Bulgaria (he was especially impressed with Constantinople). He was the sort who remembered feast days and other important events with a warm note.

Out of sight, he was not out of mind. Various friends made the trip on the fabled *Orient Express* to visit the hospitable bishop when he finally got larger quarters. And when in Rome for the prescribed formal in-person reports, he liked to entertain his clerical friends. These gestures were not with any motives of gaining favor or advancement. On the contrary, he wrote family, "I escaped willingly from [Rome] where the sight of many little moral miseries vexed me. Everybody is occupied in the search of and chattering about posts and careers. Ah! It's a poor priestly life that reduces itself to seeking such things rather than the Lord's glory and the coming of His reign." And he asked prayers that he would "always keep… far from ecclesiastical ambitions."[13]

As 1932 closed, a new lively, young priest secretary arrived. This was a youth in whom Roncalli had previously taken an interest. Ordained just a year, twenty-three-year-old Giacomo (often confused with but not even related to fellow Bergamo priest Gustavo) Testa was "good, humble… and full of eagerness to do good," as Johnine biographer Mario Benigni put it.[14] This kindred soul, like Roncalli, emphasized what unites rather than divides, looked at situations optimistically and believed good can conquer evil. For Roncalli, living with Don Giacomo was a joy.

AN END AT LAST

When he reported in person to Rome in 1934, Roncalli's friends chided him, as they had for a long time, for not complaining. They pushed him to protest that nobody else had been left for a decade in a backwater and with so little power. But Angelo Roncalli had long been a man with one concern alone: remaining in the center of God's will.

Pius XI took note. Announcing a new posting for Roncalli, he said, "We want to give Bishop Roncalli a special sign of esteem and trust because, by not asking anything for himself, he has enlightened us a great deal. Even in the last audience we did not succeed in drawing from his lips a single word expressing personal discomfort, complaint, or even a desire to be transferred after ten years of such a difficult life."[15] Then Pius named Roncalli apostolic delegate to Greece and Turkey.

Papal delegate Roncalli had long called the difficult people he served "my Bulgarians." His 1934 midnight Mass goodbye was memorable, vouching that no matter where in the world he was, there would always be a lamp in his window for Bulgarians. "You won't be asked if you are Catholic or Orthodox," he promised. "[If you are] a Bulgarian brother it's enough."[16]

He left knowing much about political and religious machinations and about being a hated and feared religious minority; at the same time he had formed positive personal relationships with a number of Orthodox leaders by the diplomacy of brotherly love.

❧ 8 ❧

Turkey and Greece

YEARS EARLIER, WHEN HE WAS PROMOTED TO ROME, THE
new Monsignor Roncalli had to leave lifelong family and
Bergamo relationships; named an archbishop meant the
greater losses of exile in Bulgaria, especially giving up his sisters' companionship. Now as he got a better posting, his
favorite nephew, about to enter the minor seminary, died.
Roncalli's view: God wanted every rose in his life to come
with thorns to keep his ego in check and spiritually focused.
To Gustavo Testa he wrote: "Secretly and in silence,... I have
shed...tears. I loved him very much."[1]

TURKEY
Since its revolution in 1922, Turkey was secularized, a republic under Kemal Ataturk in which men had to cease wearing
their beloved fezzes, and women, freed from veils, voted and
could hold office. Christians had been there from the faith's

beginnings, but twelve years after the revolution, when Roncalli arrived in January 1935, to be Turkish was to be Muslim. Under Ataturk Muslims had gained power while non-Muslims' positions had worsened.

A better post, Turkey was still no prize. Roncalli was not officially recognized by the government, had to wear secular dress in public, and a decade later government official Numan Menemencioglu told France's foreign minister, Georges Bidault: "We did everything we could to thwart him," then added, "but we never succeeded."

They did not succeed because Archbishop Roncalli had learned in Bulgaria to be like those Old Testament heroes who walked, praising God, in the furnace. He could live with the difficult situations life kept throwing at him.

His letters home characteristically brimmed with enthusiasm. He loved beautiful, cosmopolitan Constantinople, which Ataturk had renamed Istanbul in 1930. He loved having a cathedral, some priests to father and a little flock—about thirty thousand Roman rite Catholics, most in Istanbul—for whom he could "do the work of a priest."[2] He loved that little flock in spite of the facts: Most were foreigners; they didn't want to learn Turkish and felt superior to Turks; there were no Turkish priests; and the mostly Italian and French priests serving Roman rite Catholics were locked in unbrotherly power struggles, while the various Eastern rite Catholics—Armenians, Chaldeans, Syrians, Melchites, Georgians and Greco-Byzantines—weren't keen on each other either.

The archbishop introduced a little Turkish into the service, although not into the Mass itself, which was then said worldwide in Latin. He got only flack.

Thwarted and unsupported he might be, yet in the twenty-first century *One* magazine would report that "he remains a respected and beloved figure in Turkish society."[3]

Why? Because his aim was never to make Roncalli loved but to serve souls and to foster love for Christ, the pope and the Church. To these ends he used his charitable ingenuity to lessen divisions, promoting brotherhood and charity between feuding Christians as well as between Christians and Muslims. The Turks eventually took note, as Menemencioglu put it, that Roncalli "understands us and is worthy of our esteem."

SETTLING IN

Whether it was the peasant instinct to improve property or gifts that might have made him an architect or decorator, it was always Roncalli's joy to make places—none of which he would ever own—more livable and beautiful. On moving to his new quarters in Istanbul, Roncalli immediately set his Italian steward, Luigi, and two new housekeeping nuns to cleaning, while he himself weeded out furniture in bad condition. Carpenters and painters were hired with particular care for the little chapel. Over its door he had them inscribe, "To Jesus Through Mary."

The beloved now-monsignor Giacomo Testa accompanied him, but by February there was a new secretary. From Milan, ordained there six years earlier, thirty-two-year-old Angelo Dell'Acqua proved another compatible spirit whom one day Roncalli would make an archbishop—and Paul VI a cardinal.

There would be other secretaries in the next years, while Giacomo would come and go (doing advanced studies, for one thing), evoking acceptance at leave-taking and joy when he returned.

On July 28, 1935, Roncalli's father, Giovanni Battista Roncalli, died of pneumonia at age eighty-one. His archbishop son had no secretary just then to leave in charge and had to stay put. From Turkey telegrams, then letters, expressing his sorrow went to his mother and the family. He counseled taking comfort "in hope of celestial joys" when all the Roncallis would be reunited in heaven.[4]

People loved this new archbishop, and to honor his father was to honor him, so Battista received a brilliant requiem Mass in Istanbul, with all the Catholic clergy and religious present and a choir of seventy-five. The archbishop still felt a bereft child. Shutting himself in his room, he sobbed or wept, and prayed alone in his chapel. He felt it physically as well, where his emotional upsets always settled: in his stomach. A priest friend's arrival from home brought needed comfort.

In 1936 he was in Rome when the Fascists invaded Ethiopia. Roncalli wrote, in a letter dated May 24, that the success of Mussolini "makes it seem that a hidden force is guiding him and protecting Italy. Perhaps it is a reward for having made peace with the church, perhaps it is an invitation from Providence [he refers to the dictator whom he has called 'wicked'] always to live better."[5]

In 1993 some journalists would label Roncalli pro-Fascist. But that was to take these comments and others out of the context of Roncalli's criticisms of man and movement. In a sermon on February 11, 1954, the twenty-fifth anniversary of the signing of the Lateran Pacts, Roncalli summed Mussolini up thusly: Providence placed him in the path of Pius XI, because Mussolini was able to go beyond old ideas and reconcile Italy and the Church through the Lateran Pacts. "This same man later became a cause of great sorrow to the Italian people. It would be inhuman and unChristian to deprive him of this title of honour [concerning the Lateran] despite the immense calamity he [afterward] brought upon us."[6]

The whole discussion on Roncalli and Fascism can be concluded with the commonsense reminder that to be holy is not to be omniscient. In 1939 Roncalli applauded Mussolini for keeping Italy out of World War II, only to see the dictator lead the country into the conflict in 1940.

GREECE

The death of his father and the demands of his pastoral and diplomatic works kept him occupied. Only in April 1936 was he able to travel to Turkey's great historical enemy, Greece, the other part of his papal assignment. The two nations had been in armed conflict only sixteen years earlier (Turkey won). Hit by the worldwide depression of the 1930s, Greece was very poor, as was Turkey, but unlike Turkey, Greece had political and other crises, some the aftermath of the horrors of World War I. These included having to economically absorb 1,250,000 Greeks repatriated by treaty from Turkey, while only 400,000 ethnic Turks left.

Roncalli was received by a basically powerless king. Sadly, even more than in Bulgaria, the Greek Orthodox, whose painful experiences of Catholic rape, pillage and murder went all the way back to the Crusades, looked at

Catholics not as fellow Christians but as foreigners. And as foreigners went, *Italian* was perhaps as dirty a word as *Catholic* just then, Italians in 1923 having bombed and occupied a Greek island, killing many.

Roncalli could get only a tourist visa until Pius XI, after a year, sent a congratulatory letter—carried by Roncalli—to a Greek king on his installation. Suddenly the passport issue was resolved. But he still worked fruitlessly with men who, usually in velvet gloves, stymied his every effort toward Vatican diplomatic relations with Greece. Equally stymied were Roncalli's efforts toward at least rapport, if not reunion, with the Orthodox.

It all made Roncalli sigh over Greece as the most bitter and most painful part of his work for the Holy See. Fortunately, he could write a niece that his aversion to Greece was exceeded by his consolation in doing God's will, not his own. A good thing, because his dream that Greece would accept a permanent papal representative so that he could confine himself to Turkey, where he was happy, would not come true.

He contrasted the Turks, who were open about their opposition to other faiths, with the Greek Orthodox, who spoke sweetly but whose acts were driven by fear of the pope. However tried, Rome's delegate knew it was better to practice what was becoming his storied patience because, as he wrote home, "a single outburst can jeopardize everything."[7]

The 1936 trip lasted only about ten days. Roncalli was a papal delegate in Greece, not an apostolic administrator who would pastor a flock as in Turkey. Nevertheless, he wanted to visit and encourage the small scattered groups of Catholics.

So he visited the first few of Greece's many islands.

In 1937, on three Greek trips, he visited many more areas (and would visit still more in May and November of 1938) and, with his love of history, enjoyed some archaeological excursions. He also made the celebrated trip to Mount Athos. Traveling among the monasteries in this roadless area for three days, five hours a day on mule or horse, he wrote his mother of frequently asking the family's dead members and Saint Joseph to pray for him that he wouldn't fall off.

SACRIFICES: HEALTH AND FAMILY
The archbishop credited roughing it on his Greek trip with improvement in some uremic swelling, but returning to Turkey, he came down with nephritis after renal colic only five months earlier. Good Turkish doctors and loving care by his visiting sisters cured him.

It is a fact, as he noted on a retreat in 1940, that as he approached sixty he couldn't take proper care of himself. He knew he needed more sleep, regular walks and so forth. His life was overly sedentary, and he ate either catch-as-catch-can on long and often arduous journeys or too richly on what was put before him on the diplomatic circuit. He wrote home about diets, including humorously in one letter that advice to give up meat, wine and bread meant "eat like a peasant," while the recommendation of yogurt equaled "become an infant." He happily reported occasional weight losses, but overall, with his stresses and a life where the content of so many meals was outside his control, he would become increasingly rotund.

What helped him deal with physical problems like the nephritis, as with many saints, was his soul's health. In his journal he reported that going to confession gave him "renewed physical vigour and energy."[8]

Winter 1938–1939 proved a succession of deaths for Roncalli, including personal losses, even as the political climate darkened and malignant cells of war multiplied in body politics weakened from a near decade of economic miseries. In November 1938 he learned a young, married niece had died. That same month the founder of the Turkish Republic, Ataturk, died. The papal delegate was in the land of Turkey's enemy, Greece, at the time and could only send Giacomo Testa to represent the Church. This was not the best diplomatic move, even—maybe especially—for an unaccredited diplomat.

Also that November the priest friend who had come to comfort him when his father died, and who had been collaborating with him on research for Roncalli's book on Saint Charles Borromeo, died while saying Mass. "O what a blow for me!" Roncalli confided in a letter home.[9]

On February 10, 1939, Pius XI died. In the midst of all the diplomatic events the death of a pope triggers, making it absolutely impossible to go home, his dearly loved mother suddenly became gravely ill and died.

A LIGHT IN THE DARKNESS

One huge reason to remain at his post related to the Orthodox. Since 1054, when the Great Schism broke the Church into East and West, Catholics and Orthodox had resolutely closed their eyes to each other's sorrows and joys. But

Roncalli invited Orthodox leaders to ceremonies relating to the pope's death. In fact, it was said that he set up the events predominantly with an eye to rapport with the Orthodox.

He did the same at the papal election of Eugenio Pacelli, who took the name Pius XII. Possibly this was the first time since 1054 that the Orthodox Church had been advised of the election of a new pontiff.

And there was fruit: May 27, 1939, Roncalli was officially received—with ceremony and honor—by the Orthodox patriarch in Istanbul. An elated Roncalli felt he was at his best and reported, "The patriarch responded with sincerity and warmth."[10] They spoke of the work for peace of all religious groups in those anxious days of a world teetering toward war. Tactfully, they did not discuss Orthodox-Catholic union, a dream that must await a future time of grace.

❧ 9 ❧

Walking World War II's Tightrope

IN SEPTEMBER 1939 MORAL DARKNESS FELL ON EUROPE AS Nazi Germany invaded Poland. Unbidden, Roncalli organized relief for the Poles, perhaps influenced by a sobering meeting with fleeing Polish Jews. Turkey being neutral, the Vatican designated him its point of contact for the Church in Syria, Persia, Palestine, Mesopotamia, India and all Africa.

Greece also tried to stay neutral, but the Italians invaded in 1940. The Greeks held off the invaders until spring 1941, when the troops of Mussolini's German ally arrived. Hitler's bombs and tanks crushed the Greek forces, and resistance had to go underground.

Travel between Greece and Turkey became extremely arduous, but Roncalli made many trips. With prayer and a resolution to die if necessary, he traveled now most often by air, usually in German Luftwaffe military planes, German permission being required to travel into Greece. Stranded occasionally in Bulgaria, he was made much of by the royals and, when necessary, loaned car and chauffeur for his perilous travel.[1]

His was a tightrope act, reaching out to all sides in the conflict, according to his resolution: "I must be the bishop of all,...father, light, encouragement for all."[2] He said Mass for, baptized, confirmed, heard confessions and visited Greece's occupying Italian troops. He did what he could to alleviate the terrible sufferings of the thirty-five thousand or so Greek Catholics now seen by many fellow Greeks as enemy collaborators. Germans also he treated as his spiritual sons and brothers, even after Italy went over to the Allied side.

A BISHOP FOR EVERYONE

For the suffering Greek nation, he worked without end. Famine raising its skeletal head led to Roncalli's being received by and establishing at least momentary rapport with the Greek Orthodox metropolitan, willing to cooperate even with Catholics if the pope could get food to his people. Pius XII tried, but even papal efforts would not convince the blockading British and Allies to let in grain ships, lest these benefit the German occupiers. Roncalli in 1942 wrote home: "Ah Greece is a field of despair.... Hunger is something horrible...to endure.... Many old people and children...are dying from weakness. I foresee a spring that will be even more painful.... Together with...[Giacomo] Testa I have organized several works for assistance. The Holy Father has sent me half a million lire to begin with. But we will need the gift of miracles."[3]

Leaving Giacomo in charge to return to his Turkish duties, he pulled one off: a "milk fund" in Istanbul for the starving children of Greece. From his Catholic flock and Turkish Muslims—two groups who didn't like Orthodox or Greeks—he collected the then huge equivalent of a hundred thousand lire to save the starving children of people who detested Catholics, Muslims, Turks and their Italian invaders.

Besides famine relief and running a communications hub for many countries with the Vatican, his diplomatic duties continued and even, at times, intensified. But he fit in other works of compassion, his own and those he carried out on behalf of the Church.

Throughout the war Pius XII was greatly praised by *The New York Times*; the state of Israel; leading Jews of the era, from Golda Meir to Albert Einstein and the world in general for his efforts to help Jews. The pope's secretary and confidant later testified that Pius XII spent his entire inherited Pacelli family fortune to this end.[4] But efforts had to become ever more diplomatic and secret to avoid heartbreakingly counterproductive reprisals like that in the Netherlands where the Church strongly denounced anti-Semitic persecution from every Catholic pulpit with savage ongoing reprisals against Jews.[5]

Archbishop Roncalli, too, was trying to save Jews, and turned often to Pius XII, receiving what Roncalli later attested was "intervention [that was] often efficacious, always positive, and constant."[6]

The Church's man in Turkey was always trying to get what his Jewish collaborators wanted from the Vatican. These collaborators included a man Roncalli described as "warm, affable,"[7] Jerusalem's chief rabbi, Isaac Herzog. Others were Turkey's Zionist leader Chaim Barlas and Istanbul's great educator and chief rabbi for the Askenazic community, Doctor David Markus, a refugee himself from czarist Russia in 1900.

Roncalli had both successes and failures for many reasons, some having nothing to do with anti-Semitism. For instance, some in the Church didn't want Jews to get to Palestine lest they form a state there. In their concern that the Church's holy places would suffer if Jews ruled Palestine, these so-called anti-Zionists were blind to the human lives at stake if Jews fleeing Hitler were turned away from Palestine.

There was also the idea—oddly enough shared by some devout Jews—that if God had permitted their dispersal, Jews should not reestablish in Israel. Roncalli appeared to share this view, but when ideology bumped against human beings who needed help, there was no contest: Roncalli's human sympathies were unfailing; he was deeply moved by the Jews' plight.

One poignant example: Pius had Roncalli help trace the missing, a humanitarian undertaking for those on both sides of the war. A French nun wrote him from Romania in 1943 on behalf of her Jewish friend concerned about a daughter who had sailed for Israel. Reporting back to her the tragic news of the ship's sinking with only one male survivor, Roncalli exclaimed: "Poor children of Israel! Every day I hear their groans all around me. I mourn with them and do my best to help them. They are the relatives and countrymen of Jesus. May the Divine Savior come to their aid."[8]

CLANDESTINE EFFORTS

In Greece that prayer was answered through efforts by energetic young Monsignor Giacomo Testa. Other thousands of Jews from Slovakia, now in Bulgaria and in danger of arrest, as well as Jews in Romania and Hungary were trying to escape via neutral Turkey to the Holy Land. For those in Bulgaria, Roncalli appealed to King Boris, whose fear of his homegrown Communists and Russia had made him an uneasy ally of Nazi Germany. (He had tried to move secretly to the Allied side but was told he had to accept not just America and Britain but Russia— death to a free Bulgaria.)

Rather than arguing against the anti-Semitic propaganda circulating in Bulgaria, the archbishop agreed that "some sons of Judah are not faultless, [although] there are also many innocent persons." Then he appealed to Boris's faith and his ego: Helping the Jews would bring "great honor...to the dignity of a Christian sovereign." And finally—knowing Boris's heavy anxieties—he assured him such deeds "would become before the God of mercy a promise of blessings during these times of trial."[9]

Boris did as Roncalli asked, and thousands of Slovakians got transit visas for Palestine. Perhaps this good deed weighed in the eternal balance when the king mysteriously died "like a saint," as Queen Giovanna wrote Roncalli in 1943, almost certainly himself a war victim.[10]

One way Roncalli helped Jews get out of Hungary and Romania was by issuing certificates of immigration. (Later, those wanting to show Roncalli's goodness mistakenly called them baptismal certificates.) He distributed them in Budapest through Hungary's papal nuncio, Archbishop Angelo Rotta, and in Romania through that nation's nuncio, Archbishop Andrea Cassulo. Other Romanian collaborators included the ecumenically minded Sisters of Our Lady of Sion.

In a time of war, stationed in one country that was neutral and in another occupied by the Nazis, a smart man did not publicize what he was doing to save Jews. And Roncalli was tight-lipped about his good deeds anyway, unless he could credit them to the pope. But many years later, when he *was* pope, he shared with a Jewish group from America what it meant to him when, as papal delegate, he learned of a ship carrying several thousand Jewish children directly into Nazi hands and was able to quietly reroute it.

In all his efforts he sought to overcome evil with good and live the belief he expressed in signing a letter to Zionist leader Chaim Barlas, "Ever at your service and at the service of all the *brothers* of Israel" (emphasis added).[11]

THE NAZIS' MAN?

Although Roncalli was celebrated publicly in a small way among the Jews as a Nazi opponent for a sermon denouncing racism, like Pius he worked primarily behind the scenes. Had he denounced the Nazis, he would have either been "eliminated" by their agents in Istanbul or forbidden entry to Greece, where he was doing so much good. As it was, the Third Reich's diplomat in Turkey, German aristocrat Franz von Papen, funneled information the Nazis wanted the Vatican to believe through naïve-appearing or naïve Roncalli, depending on one's point of view. Roncalli passed on what von Papen told him, and the Vatican recipients thought Roncalli naïve as well.

Roncalli kept his counsel, but when secret maneuvers were needed to save Jews, just as he went confidently to Turks to help enemy Greeks, he went to the German Catholic representative of the Nazis, asked for von Papen's help and received it. Years later, under oath for the beatification process, von Papen could say from personal knowledge—"personal" because von Papen had been involved—that Roncalli had aided twenty-four thousand Jews.

As the war turned against the Nazis, von Papen was ordered back to Germany. At the first stop on his train journey, there was Roncalli come to say good-bye. The German diplomat, absolutely certain that if he escaped being shot by the Nazis he would be hung by the Allies, knelt on the platform and asked Roncalli's blessing.

He got it—and more. Some years later as a charged "war criminal" at the Nuremberg Trials he was acquitted, thanks to a letter from Roncalli citing von Papen's role in rescuing Jews. Von Papen testified years later to Roncalli's great spirituality, his ecumenism and his generosity toward the persecuted.[12] He meant the Jews but could have referred to himself.

Pius XII appealed to Roncalli for word on the Italian soldiers who, as Germany pulled back and Russia advanced, were being captured by the Communists. Roncalli brought his usual commitment to the task. Leaving not a diplomatic or personal avenue untried, he had to report back an unbreachable information barrier. Not too much later the world would name this Communist barrier the Iron Curtain.

"TWIN STARS"
United in apostolic fire and depth of spirituality, there had been an immediate meeting of hearts, minds and, it is not too

much to say, souls when Roncalli met the sixteen-years-younger Giovanni Battista Montini in Fascist-imperiled Rome in 1924. In 1925 peasant-born Roncalli had received a congratulatory letter from Montini, son of one of Italy's important families, when Roncalli was named an archbishop. A good-bye visit before Roncalli's departure for Bulgaria followed.

Fourteen years later, in June 1938, Roncalli penned a letter of both saint's day greetings and congratulations to his soul friend when Montini was named Pius XII's undersecretary of state. In reply Montini wrote his thanks for the esteem, the devotion and the affection he read in Roncalli, citing the letter's "true expression of the exquisite goodness of your soul." He added that he "very often thinks of the difficulties in which Your Excellency finds yourself."[13]

They exchanged letters on the famine in Greece, the conversations with von Papen (Montini, too, judged his friend naïve) and many other matters pertinent to their positions. Although separated most of their lives, their friendship would last throughout, and their letters fill a book. These letters were sometimes touching, sometimes almost comically obsequious as each tried to efface himself to show the depth of his esteem for the other man. "Like certain twin stars who move in the same orbit," said Archbishop Capovilla, who knew both, the friends would remain side by side in soul, and one day the younger would succeed the older as pope.[14]

TAKING STOCK

On his 1940 six-day retreat at the Sisters of Sion house on the Bosporus, considering himself moving into old age (he would turn sixty on November 25, 1941), Roncalli took stock. Some of his conclusions:

On his family: It was certainly right not just to love them but to help them financially "when their poverty makes this necessary [always from his own stipend, never Church money] when he does so much to help strangers." But he must do this "in a priestly, impartial manner," without getting involved in family affairs in a way that would divert him from his calling.

On sex: Age brought not complete freedom but some welcome withering of sexual desires, and he was grateful for this comparative "silence and tranquility of the flesh" after "the temptations which disturbed it in the years of my youth and vigorous maturity." He warned himself, nonetheless, that it was still possible to become "the foolish, doting old man."[15]

On money: "This year Providence has placed considerable sums of money in my hands for my own personal use. I have distributed it all." He cited expenditures on the poor, his family's needs and a few personal ones, and using most of the funds to restore the Church properties he lived in and rooms elsewhere for "some of my priests." He summed up: "According to this world's judgments…and…human prudence, I have been a fool. In fact, now I am poor again. Blessed be the Lord. I think that by his grace, I did the right thing. Again I trust in his generosity for the future. 'Give and it shall be given unto you.' "[16]

On war: "Desired by men, deliberately…is what makes it so evil."[17] He also ruminated on the difference between patriotism and nationalism and prayed to be saved from the latter, as well as noting the hypocrisy of nations who violate God's laws to go to war, then expect God to spare them war's consequences.[18]

On himself: It was now forty years since his 1900 resolution not to sin deliberately. He had kept it. But there was no self-righteous self-congratulating. He journaled at length about sharing the human proclivity to sin and his need to always appreciate the greatness of God's mercy and the grace poured out abundantly on him in spite of his unworthiness. But he also recognized growth, seeing "something more mature and authoritative in me,...a greater detachment from all that concerns my own future, a more marked indifference 'to all created things,'...a more evident inclination to understand and sympathize and a greater clarity and tranquility in impressions and judgments."[19]

On two personality traits and suffering: A few small lies told in his childhood "have left in my heart a horror of deceit and falsehood." He gave gratitude to God—and prayed to continue in—"a natural inclination to tell the truth,...in all circumstances before everyone, in a pleasant manner and with courtesy, to be sure, but calmly and fearlessly."[20]

He also gave thanks for his inborn "happy nature," which had spared him many afflictions. But the man who followed Christ did not expect a life without any suffering. "It is only to be expected, that, before the end of my humble life, the Lord will send me trials of a particularly painful nature. Well, I am ready: provided that the Lord...grant me the strength to bear them with calm, dignity, and sweetness."[21]

Meantime, he pledged himself to teach, by word and example, God's truth and mercy to all.[22]

1944: ENDS AND BEGINNINGS

Finally, in 1944, the war began winding down, bringing tremendous changes for this part of the world.

Defeat in their tracks, that September the Nazis pulled out of the Balkans. In Bulgaria they abandoned the little six-year-old king, Boris's son Simeon, through whom they had ruled with puppet regents. As the dreaded Russians invaded, Queen Giovanna escaped the country with the tyke and his sister. Boris's old Communist enemies emerged with plans to improve education, health and social services, to pay back enemies and to crush any political opposition—and all religion. Orthodox and Catholic would finally unite in something: shedding their blood for Christ.

Suffering Greece, whose largest, most effective of several resistance movements was Communist-led, plunged into fierce and bloody civil war when her invaders left. But by Christmastime the country would be in a temporary peace with anti-Communists in power through British and American help.

Well-governed, stable, Muslim Turkey, having escaped all threats of Nazi invasion, diplomatically joined the winning side when there was no possibility of reprisal, only to face new peril from her Russian neighbor: Postwar aims of the Communist superpower included controlling the portion of Turkey that sat in Eastern Europe and setting up military bases in the country. As 1944 ended, no one knew how or if the Turks would escape.

Changes were brewing for Roncalli too.

❧ 10 ❧

The Paris Years

ON DECEMBER 6, 1944, A SECRET VATICAN MESSAGE ARRIVED. Chosen not by committee but by Pius XII—"I myself thought, prayed, and decided"[1] Pius would tell him in person before the month was out—Turkey's lowly, unrecognized Church diplomat was being named nuncio in Paris, *crème de la crème* of diplomatic posts.

Nuncios are the top-ranking Vatican ambassadors.

This was a "clap of thunder" as Roncalli described it, but his motto, "Obedience and Peace," steadied him to simply accept.

He experienced sorrow in leaving Turkey, which he loved. There was no time for big, public occasions where he could express his regrets over leaving people, places and ministries because Rome announced his selection only on December 22, with orders to leave at once. He managed what personal good-byes he could fit in and a banquet for his clergy on December 23, the day he departed for Ankara, and a few days' protocol-demanded, diplomatic farewells.

A French government plane rushed Roncalli to Paris on December 30, after a one-day briefing in Rome. Conflict between Pius XII and the provisional postwar government of Charles de Gaulle had led to withdrawing the nuncio. But even in their conflict, Pius and de Gaulle agreed: When, as on every December 31, the dean of the diplomatic corps offered France's leader New Year's greetings for 1945, the dean must, as always, be the papal nuncio. Because if not, the honor would pass to the oldest member of the corps, and the oldest at that moment represented Communist Russia, nemesis of the Church *and* of de Gaulle.

Roncalli arrived in time, read diplomatically proper greetings to de Gaulle and was cordial to the Russian. Crisis resolved.

As for the Pius–French government squabble, no one expected that to be solved overnight, even by the most cordial nuncio. For one thing, before going out and about, a minor crisis of Roncalli's own needed resolving. Rushed through Rome, he had left an order there for new clerical garments. Under Turkish antireligious regulations, he had been wearing suits with his Roman collar, while putting on weight. Now from the world's center of sartorial elegance and refinement, Roncalli sent an SOS to his friend, the future Paul VI. Could Montini urge the tailor to hurry since Roncalli's need for the new clothing was "more or less extreme"?[2] The future pope noted on the pleading letter of the other future pope that the goods were on the way.

A DELICATE TASK

Postwar Paris sounded like a much easier assignment than Roncalli's past posts. Although he lamented the lack of pastoral work, he would deal with one country, one principal liturgical rite, one language, one nationality. First, however, he had to face and heal the disunity between the pope and the new postwar French government that had led to his predecessor's withdrawal.

The new government was demanding removal of twenty-five bishops accused of collaboration with France's Petain government during the Nazis' occupation. Pius's orders to Roncalli were to stave off these dismissals. The new nuncio was also to maintain Church independence with those who desired Resistance priest-heroes fill the vacated seats. Pius XII's stand was that it was for the Church—not governments—to decide who was dismissed and who appointed her bishops.

Archbishop Roncalli was told it was not the government but Resistance Catholics who wanted held accountable those bishops who had remained silent or made statements that caused crises of conscience for people risking their lives against the Nazis. If nothing was done, warned André Latreille, the Ministry of Internal Affairs' Liaison to religious groups, the result would be "a disdainful indifference" toward the Church and "revival of anti-clericalism."[3]

Roncalli practiced "the grand diplomacy of evangelical charity." According to Giacomo Testa's assessment, quoted by Capovilla, "his smiling goodness, his calm, his patience, his firm steadiness, and his ability to turn around and surmount obstacles" saved the Church from catastrophe.[4] By July, with help from others, the matter was settled with the dismissal, without fanfare or censure, of seven bishops due to "resignation" or "health issues."

Having been busy getting to know the nation's clergy, Roncalli nominated men for the empty seats on the basis of being "good and holy,... dedicated completely to the sanctification of souls, beyond any political concern."[5] Men of this type, he believed, would be the best security "for the resurrection of France."[6]

Those in France's government generally scorned Roncalli's nominations. A November 1945 government report interpreted his choices as "candidates whose mediocrity is a guarantee of their total obedience to... [Rome]."[7] With no public reprimand by the Church of those bishops believed collaborators and no new bishops from among the Resistance heroes, the Catholic public, the report said, was disappointed and agitated.[8] Roncalli had found no documentation of any of the collaboration accusations, but he and Pius may have fumbled in foresight in not choosing at least one of the Resistance heroes.

WHEN WOULD THE WAR END?
Although he would never defend himself nor criticize the government except in his diary, Roncalli could find the French government lacking in foresight too. For their own future good, the French needed reconciliation with neighbor Germany. Yet they had camps full of Germans—"the least responsible"[9] simple soldiers, an exasperated Roncalli sighed—and showed no sign of letting these poor POWs go home. As early as April 1945, barely done helping Jews

escape the German Nazi regime, Roncalli was working with a saintly German priest, Abbé Franz Stock, to aid the over 260,000 German POWs.

By September 1945, helped by generous priest-professors from Germany, the five hundred seminarians among fifteen thousand Germans at a Chartres POW camp resumed their studies in camp. Roncalli would ordain two of them in 1947. His September 1945 diary entry after a camp visit: "The condition of forty undernourished, walking skeletons broke my heart!"

That Christmas he distributed gifts from the pope to German prisoners in a military hospital. February 22, 1946, a plaint in his diary after another camp visit: "Why don't they let them go free!" Even in 1948, the diary noted, he was still visiting POWs, doing what he could for them and leaving their camps "with a heavy heart."[10]

THE HIGH LIFE

Representing the pope to the government as much as to the Church in France, the nuncio attended state and cultural events, as well as events hosted by other ambassadors on behalf of their nations. And like other ambassadors, Roncalli entertained. Guests included government officials, other VIPs and the diplomatic corps, for such papal landmarks as Pius XII's anniversary of election to the papacy.

Unlike the usual ambassador, Roncalli feted non-VIPS and the poor too. On the fifty-year jubilee of Pius's priesthood, in April 1949, the nuncio, after celebrating Mass, provided a special meal to three thousand people above the age of seventy.[11] For the 1950 Holy Year, he sent money from Pius to each bishop, to use for his poorest priests and most miserable children, citing these as two of the pope's predilections.

Mixing with elite government and society figures (taking tea with a countess, for instance), he wrote a brother, "When I find myself... in [their] gilded palaces,... I smile a little and think of [the family home] and the simplicity of our fields and our domestic practices. And I envy no one."[12]

He knew this interior freedom was a grace, since in Paris "there is nothing lacking to tempt one."[13] He relied on the family's prayers, especially those of the children, to keep him in "simplicity, humility, and good health."[14]

Early on he was honored as dean of the diplomatic corps by the French Minister of Foreign Affairs, with what many would consider an obscenely ostentatious meal of thirty courses. Mentioning it in passing in a letter to an old friend, Roncalli reduced such worldly glitter to size by immediately turning to the gritty, tragic realities of saying Mass before a crowd of "tens of thousands" gathered on the vast esplanade from the ancient Trocadero to the Eiffel Tower: survivors from the German death (and other) camps, a throng of widows of those who perished and around a hundred priests distributing Communion dressed in their prison uniforms.[15]

For him the high life was ordaining forty-nine priests in the city's Notre Dame Cathedral on June 29, 1949, most of them survivors of death or labor camps. "Several times," he wrote in his diary, "I was nearly overcome by emotion."[16] Such events, not strictly duties of the nuncio, balanced his diplomatic round.

Things that *were* Church duties, besides long reports to Rome on various matters, included presiding over new bishops' installations; marking individual jubilees of cardinals, archbishops, bishops and other important Church figures; as well as entertaining churchmen visiting from other countries.

His own ego he kept well squashed, writing in 1950: "I represent the Holy Father and the interests of the Holy Church in France.... Where does my poor self enter in?"[17] His answer: not at all. When young, one of his faults was interjecting his opinions inappropriately. Now he elicited the comment that no one knew where Roncalli himself stood on things, such as the controversial worker-priests sent into France's factories by Cardinal Emmanuel Suhard in hopes of winning workers back from the Communists. Roncalli would be for these worker-priests when Rome was and draw back when Rome did.

Again he practiced his loving diplomacy with the Church's adversaries during a drawn-out conflict over whether the government should finance students in Catholic schools. In the end he could rejoice because the votes were there to keep Catholic school doors open.

THE CALL OF DUTY—AND BEYOND

Examining his calendar from the French years, one sees that he took on roughly a dozen special occasions each month; that's one every two to three days, not a few requiring arduous travel. A sampling: He visited an orphanage, met with Catholic students at the Sorbonne, welcomed a foreign cardinal to a French Eucharistic Congress, celebrated a special anniversary of one of his heavenly role models, seventeenth-century French Bishop Saint Francis de Sales, and presided over the dedication of the Basilica of Saint Thérèse in Lisieux. Among several other Thérèsian events during his Paris years, he was in Lisieux to honor Thérèse's seventy-eight-year-old blood sister Celine (Soeur Genevieve) on the fiftieth anniversary of her Carmelite vows. While there he met the only other living sister of the saint, Pauline (Mère Agnes), Carmel's prioress, who would die in 1951, just before her ninetieth birthday.

He presided over First Communions and confirmations at churches all over the country and opened the 1947 International Congress of Young Catholic Students in Pontoise. In France's African colony Algeria, he spoke positively of both the Arab peoples and of the Jews whom he called "children of the promise," reminiscing about his exchanges of human and brotherly charity during the war. He traveled to Grenoble to say Mass for a favorite order of nuns, the Sisters of Sion, participated in a night of prayer at Montmarte, met with a group of French youth and donned an apron to serve a meal to the aged. And when there was terrible flooding in Alsace-Lorraine in May 1947, he rushed to the disaster site "to see how the Holy Father can help."[18]

Explaining his motives for keeping himself on the run like this all over France and beyond, he cited, as usual, his desire of "making the Pope and the Church loved" but also his hope, in the postwar world's tense polarization between Communism and the West, to promote peace.[19]

As the Vatican's appointed observer, he talked to the world at UNESCO (the United Nations Educational, Scientific and Cultural Organization), but most of his work for peace was person to person. For example, on one occasion he found himself in the hinterlands to welcome back from wartime hiding the relics of the area's patron saint, an event both religious and political. The mayor, of rural origin and a fervent Communist, displayed chagrin at having to greet Roncalli, representative of the hated Church. He excused himself with a snide reference to his inability to come up to the elegant expressions of the nuncio. Roncalli replied:

> It's no unhappiness for me, Monsieur Mayor, to receive the good wishes of a son of the country whom the will of the people has called to govern the community.... On the contrary, it is a great honor.... The one to whom you render honor in his position as representative of the highest spiritual authority on earth, also boasts to say he too is the son of a humble but strong and honest laborer. So let's shake hands and thank the good God who made us and whom [in civic and religious leadership] we represent.[20]

KINDNESS IS A LANGUAGE TOO

As Monsignor Capovilla put it, if the nuncio was not gifted in languages, Roncalli was still a great communicator. He had used French—diplomacy's language—in the Balkans, and he preached in it now. But humbly: Speaking at a congress of youth, for example, he asked his young listeners to overlook "the poorness of my accent" and "believe in the sincerity of my sentiments."[21]

There were some bloopers. Seeking to compliment a woman member of the diplomatic world, Roncalli called her "a public woman," a phrase very nice in Italian but which, alas, in French means a prostitute. What saved him in any faux pas was that he was so obviously well intentioned.

A heart like Roncalli's was always on call. Monsignor Capovilla described how the nuncio—worn out from all the extra events of the 1950 Holy Year—arrived in Sotto il Monte after a long, tiring journey on September 24, ready for much-needed rest. But learning that French seminarians on pilgrimage from Poitiers were hospitalized in Ravenna from a car wreck, he was at their bedsides on September 26.

It is highly unlikely, added Capovilla—with the disclaimer that he intended no reproach to anyone—that any other diplomat of either France or Italy turned up at the bedside of the youths. Capovilla's point: For the nuncio, charity way beyond normal expectations was a simple duty.[22]

The nuncio's wallet was equally "on call." Monsignor Capovilla quoted pre-beatification testimony that Roncalli went through the personal pocket money provided him so fast the priest auditor was embarrassed to submit the books to Rome with so many "alms" listings. He took it upon himself to explain to Archbishop Roncalli that the nunciate was a diplomatic undertaking, not a charity. He set limits on the monthly allowance. Roncalli could still give it away to the many who touched his heart or whom his warm compassion encouraged to put the financial touch on him. But at least the amount would not look excessive to Rome. It was a good plan, but how dry up springs of compassion? Roncalli still came to his auditor with empty pockets not far into each month.[23]

The more warmth and kindness the nuncio showed, the more he was loved. This led to more invitations. He should stay home and not go running all over France was the criticism of some—in both government and Church—unused to this kind of diplomacy.

Roncalli was called to a meeting with Pius XII, who expressed his displeasure that France's nuncio was absent from his nunciate so much. Roncalli wrote in his diary on September 27, 1946, that he was grateful to have been humbled by the pope and grateful that Pius humbled him so little. The entry noted he gave a respectful explanation but no insistence on his own defense.

He also noted both that pleasing the Holy Father was the only important thing and that the bishops, priests and laypeople wanted him to accept their invitations. Roncalli chose to accommodate Pius XII's desires, but in what must be called a mystery, the calendar remained just as full. And there was no more disciplining of the nuncio.

A TOUCH OF CLASS

Roncalli's love of improving the places where he lived melded with his desire to express his filial love for the pope. He hired a renowned—but "inexpensive," he noted in his letter to Pius—Italian painter to improve the nunciature's drab dining room with ceiling murals.

With the help of a benefactor, he also bought five fine wall hangings in great need of repair, for which he commissioned French Franciscan nuns who specialized in that type of restoration. When his research discovered that two of the hangings were part of an extremely valuable group called the *Collezione Barberiniana* in the Vatican Museums, he donated them in exchange for two lesser tapestries, still fine enough to add the right touch of elegance to the dining room. And to leave him, once again, in personal poverty.

Because of his Franciscan simplicity and humility, sometimes lost to view was the side of Roncalli that, in his seminary days, admired the priests who "knew everything" and went at his studies intently to emulate them.[24] It was this cultured and learned man who loved the fine arts, buying tapestries, Persian carpets and religious paintings for the Sotto il Monte church, the Bergamo seminary, papal residences such as the Paris nunciate and, less often, his rented Sotto il Monte vacation quarters, where he housed his sisters. He never felt conflicted about his personal commitment to poverty and the necessity to furnish residences where bishops and government representatives were to be entertained, even sometimes housed, with the dignity appropriate to the pope's representative.

This Roncalli was the visitor of archeological sites, a master of classical Greek and Latin, and a history scholar and author at home in archives and libraries, still trying to finish his five-part work on Saint Charles Borromeo. Besides devoting most of one vacation to the project, he made time for it by getting up extra early in Paris, carefully not stealing any hours from his nuncio duties. This Roncalli—witty, wise and knowledgeable in all these areas—Capovilla claims, held his own with French society and the diplomatic corps.

It was he who received autographed copies of their latest books—among them one dedicated to him, another a special edition just for him—from historians, from a member of the nation's language and literary watchdog, the Académie Française, and from a writer on the fine arts.

And yet in his eloquent and sensitive, beautifully written letters of thanks in French, as well as in the speeches he made to cultured groups, the nuncio did not court intellectual prestige. He let some think less of him by cheerfully quoting, along with classical works, "folksy," "uncultured" LaFontaine's fables.

The fables aren't always so Christian, he acknowledged, but they have their feet on the ground of reality.[25]

His lack of ostentation spilled over to the inner workings of the nunciate. In most embassies class and status were rigidly observed. Roncalli tried for a different atmosphere. In February 1951 he sent a typical letter home that ended with his salute to all his big family in the names of all in the nunciate: his three clerical assistants—Giacomo Testa (who had joined him in 1950), "Lambertini [and] Heim[--]Religious [sisters] and Housekeeping Staff."[26] Sometimes he listed the domestics by name. And he wrote his sisters in the summer of 1949 behind Heim's back, to have his own bedroom in Sotto il Monte ready for the Swiss monsignor, who was used to running water, a proper bathroom and all those comforts, "of which I can [easily] deprive myself."[27]

Unordinary Views

A cousin died, and even though death held no terror for Roncalli since Radini Tedeschi's end, he wrote, "O how sad. A mystery of Providence."[28] Everyone understood how death could evoke sadness even in the faith-filled, but other attitudes of the nuncio were less understandable to the world in general.

Both before and after the postwar surge of births—a brief time when children were greatly valued—having "too many" children was considered a terrible misfortune. Roncalli, however, saw every child as a family treasure, in good times or bad. The elderly were beginning to be considered a burden, but he believed the families in which they resided were blessed.

Regarding the death of good people—he wrote of his own family members—he believed any pain and suffering involved brought graces to the sufferer and the loved ones. He maintained Catholic teaching that most of the dead needed purification to be received into heaven. But looking at those exemplary Christians, his Roncalli relatives, he judged their lives as so hard that their time in purgatory would surely be minimal.

He also believed that the souls in heaven were "praying for us [whom they loved] and...assist[ing] us with love made more alive in the light of glory."[29] Finally, he counseled the living to gain graces by honoring their dead with remembrances and prayers, practices he was faithful to his entire life.

On his annual retreats during these years, he questioned once whether at least one of his good qualities was also a weakness. Generally a positive trait, his was a temperament that was not adversarial, tending to see the best in others. When he didn't find the good he sought, he schooled himself in the Golden Rule: Never say to anyone else what he wouldn't like said to him. When he saw someone on his staff treat someone—usually a lower-class or poor person—disrespectfully, he suffered deeply, was even at times tempted to react violently; but instead of taking the individual to task, he kept silent, trying to teach by example rather than upbraiding. Was this a weakness, he asked himself? Not sure, he left it to God and carried on in the same "soft" style.

Softhearted Roncalli was also known for his wit. Visiting the Académie Française, he remarked, poking fun at his girth, that the seats were sized for "a demi-nuncio."[30] Another incident was also widely reported: Asked by a fellow guest at a banquet if he was embarrassed by the scandal of Parisian socialites at the table in very low-necked attire, he twinkled, "Why, there's no scandal: nobody's looking at them; they're all too busy looking at *me* to see how the Apostolic Nuncio is taking it."[31]

"Neither a Sacrament nor a Sacramental"

On January 12, 1953, Archbishop Roncalli was officially named a cardinal of the Catholic Church. He also was decorated with France's Legion of Honor. As always when he received promotions, there was a sharp personal thorn. This time his closest sister's diagnosis with terminal stomach cancer kept his eyes fixed on the eternal. On his way from Paris to see her, he jotted in his diary: "How thankful I am that a time which could lead to temptations of vanity and self-satisfaction should become instead a period of union with the cross."[32]

To all congratulations he replied, "Being made a Cardinal is neither a sacrament nor a sacramental," meaning it had no particular spiritual value; therefore, it was of no great import. To his family he explained: It was good only if, as with Cardinal Ferrari and Pius X (whose canonization was pending), it led to sanctity and eternal salvation. He sought prayers that he would be the kind of humble, holy cardinal who did honor to the Church.[33]

There was also a new assignment that would bring him back to Italy after twenty-eight years: cardinal patriarch of Venice.

❦ 11 ❧

Shepherd of Venice

THE VENETIANS TOOK CARDINAL PATRIARCH RONCALLI TO
their hearts at once for who and what he was: simple, humble
and open to all. He had always felt that a churchman could
not be just a diplomat; he must be a shepherd of souls as well.[1]
Now, after thirty years of raising eyebrows by this unique
kind of diplomacy, he could simply *be* a shepherd.

A flotilla of small boats—the patriarch standing, blessing
the city and the people—having brought him to St. Mark's
Square Sunday afternoon, March 15, 1953, the seventy-one-
year-old new cardinal encouraged his flock from the world-
famous cathedral's pulpit to look to him that way, as a father
and a shepherd come to them in the name of the Lord.

Happily he set out to guide and guard souls in his ninety-
four parishes and to be a father to nearly 250 priests and
thirty seminarians. Although given a Fiat, he was often seen

on the flat, floating equivalent of a city bus, the *vaporetto*, or having a glass of wine at some unpretentious café in St. Mark's Square, chatting willingly with anyone who approached.

IN HOUSE AND OUT

Roncalli invited Bergamo's Sisters of the Poor to be his house-keepers, and instead of a professional chauffeur or valet, he hired twenty-three-year-old Guido Gusso from a nearby fishing village to help him with the things the sisters couldn't handle, such as accompanying him on trips, driving when necessary and tending and getting him into his patriarchal regalia. Guido would be with him to the end of his employer's life.

Don Loris Capovilla, editor of the Venetian Catholic newspaper *The Voice of San Marco*, had met Roncalli in 1950, when the Paris nuncio took part in an event in Venice. The two hit it off. Christmas cards were exchanged. Roncalli wasted no time in inviting Capovilla to be his secretary. Looking back, Capovilla said that as a priest of the diocese, he was able to help Roncalli get his bearings in Venice after years of such different work. And humbly, he volunteered, he learned much from the patriarch's shepherd's heart. They would be coworkers until Roncalli's death.

Desiring, the patriarch noted in his *Journal*, "to live and die for the souls entrusted to me,"[2] he started, with Capovilla and Guido, three years of the usual bishop's visitations to the parishes. As was traditional, the visits would be followed by a synod.

The patriarch initiated some programs and undertakings that succeeded, such as bringing the junior seminarians back to Venice. Others failed, including his attempt to open a seminary for the Eastern rite Churches on a nearby island.

If the people loved him, he was still criticized by some for a "loose" work style that did not hover over the details; but he was following many an acclaimed leader when he handed a project over to some good, capable person, better able to hew the firm line than he, and gave the individual freedom to act. Defenders might say his style was a function of a man beyond egotism, who did not have to clutch all work and credit to himself. Capovilla's view: Each man has his style, and no man is perfect in every area. Had Christ wanted perfection in the running of the Church, he would have stayed and run it himself.

Roncalli had visits from French VIP admirers such as Socialist President Vincent Auriol; devout if unconventional Catholic François Mauriac, who in 1952 won the Nobel Prize for literature; and at least twice Cardinal Maurice Feltin, one of those on the infamous list Roncalli "saved," now chief French primate. And when possible he invited old and dear friends like Montini, now archbishop of Milan, for various Church events. But no visit by these and others of the world's great kept Venice's patriarch from welcoming warmly the simplest member of his clergy or his peasant relatives from Sotto il Monte.

Getting to Sotto il Monte, except on his summer vacation, was hard. He had been able to be with neither father nor mother at their deaths; now duties again required the sacrifice of what he and the dying desired most. His one-year-older sister, the closest person to him on earth, received the last sacraments from other hands as she died on November 11,

1953. Two days later he wearily entered the house where she lived, kissed the corpse's brow and told Capovilla that this was the second kiss he had ever given her, the first being when he had learned of the cancer.

He presided at his sister's funeral and then her burial among all the other Roncallis in Sotto il Monte's cypress-lined hillside cemetery. Capovilla remembered that on the trip back to Venice, this man of great faith murmured from his cross, as the train pierced the winter gray and its wheels clacked their lonely dirge, "Woe to us if it's all an illusion."

Two months later, on January 18, 1954, the eldest Roncalli sibling, a widow, died. That year, in one brief period, the cardinal gave five funeral orations, including one for a close seminary friend. Suddenly, like autumn leaves, his generation was being swept away. The May 29 canonization of former Venetian patriarch Giuseppe Sarto, Pope Pius X—which he attended in Rome—helped keep his eyes fixed on the goals: holiness and heaven.

JUBILEE

That August was Roncalli's fiftieth year of priesthood. From World War I, when he refused a medal for his work, he had done his best to evade honors that were for him personally. He explained to his Venetians in writing that he understood their goodness and their desire to celebrate his priestly anniversary, but if they celebrated by praying for him—and he was certain they would—that was all they needed to do. He added that he had given what "was at my disposal" as donations to the seminary, to the St. Vincent de Paul Society (a worldwide lay group that aids the poor) and to certain individuals in poverty. "This is my celebration," he said in closing, "to give."[3]

Since it was summertime he was able to get home for a quiet family celebration. He journaled: "My golden jubilee.... A wonderfully bright sky after beneficial night showers. The sound of the Angelus from S. Giovanni roused me...with a 'Laus tibi, Domine' ['Praise to you, Lord']. There followed an hour of prayer.... What is my poor life after fifty years of priesthood?... My merit- -God's mercy."[4]

His giving to the poor for the jubilee was not from abundance. In a letter home he characterized himself as "a poor Cardinal who helps the poor."[5] Many previous patriarchs probably had other income than the post's pitiful stipend. Rather than raise it, he preferred "to bless the Lord for this poverty, which is rather humiliating and often embarrassing," as when he could set only a scanty table or had to endure the pain of so little to give the many who sought his help. This voluntary hidden suffering, he felt, "draws me closer to Jesus, who was poor," and blessed his ministry.[6]

A last thorn among all the deaths in his jubilee year: Before 1954's end the second of his two unmarried sisters was also diagnosed with stomach cancer. He confessed, "Ah, how terribly sad this [illness] is for me."[7] And he wrote her that he was always thinking about having two sisters who renounced families of their own to stay with him, their priest brother, and then when it seemed time for the three to finally enjoy each other's company—they could have lived with him in Venice—illness and death arrived. This sorrow turned his mind, he told his sister before her death on April 18, 1955, to the reunion in heaven, more beautiful than Venice or even Sotto il Monte.

EVERYBODY'S PATRIARCH

Capovilla insisted in interviews that he not be written of as a spiritual son but as a secretary, with the distance between two people that word implies. But that is not how Roncalli saw him. Updating his will after only a year of working together, Roncalli called Capovilla "my *beloved*, distinguished and faithful secretary, whom I shall never cease to thank on earth and in heaven for the intelligent and affectionate service which, with incomparable devotion, he has been pleased to render to me personally and to my episcopal ministry."[8]

Roncalli eventually made his personal secretary his literary executor, and Capovilla, amid his own later archbishop's duties, has dedicated his life to giving the world access to Pope John XXIII's writings, speeches, private letters, spiritual journal and so forth, through their publication and through his own writings (still only in Italian). In addition, even into his nineties, he was helping this and other Johnine biographers. The following anecdotes are Capovilla's memories. He titled them *fioretti* ("little flowers") the term used for anecdotes from Saint Francis' life due to their charm and simplicity.

Criticized for the way he ran the diocese, Roncalli was also thought less of by some for his pastoral practices with individuals. Again cited was his "looseness," phrased variously as lack of prudence, weakness or naiveté, depending on the circumstances. His critics did not see the flock from the spiritual heights where Roncalli dwelled. Capovilla quoted the view from the summit in the patriarch's words: "The bishop is responsible before God for the evangelization of everyone."[9]

Among "everyone" were some very varied souls. Capovilla recalled the young priest whom other clerics, including he, judged should have his priestly faculties suspended. Capovilla informed the patriarch that he was being criticized as weak and too malleable for not doing so. Only after they finished the pre-supper rosary was there a reply. Before saying the meal blessing, the patriarch picked up a glass from the table and asked his secretary, "Whom does this belong to?" Capovilla responded that it belonged to the householder, thus to Roncalli.

"If I let it fall to the floor, the pieces then are whose?" Answering himself, the patriarch went on, "They are still mine and I will be constrained to get down and pick them up. This priest is entrusted to me and not to them [the critics]." Then he explained to Capovilla that he had no intention of taking drastic disciplinary action until he had exhausted every avenue of charity, and the priest, by rejecting every overture, had rendered his conduct inexcusable before God and man.

The suspension was never made. "The fruit of love and grace," as Capovilla described it, Roncalli's charity apparently turned the misbehaving young priest's life around.

Capovilla also remembered an old priest, not a bad man but a sick one. He was in a rest home due to an alcohol problem. His priestly faculties suspended, he had stopped praying, was bitter and didn't want to see anyone.

The patriarch visited. His approach: "Don Giovanni, we're old, you and I; let's not forget each other, *voltiamoci* on the part of the Lord." Approached this way, the old man was convinced to take up Mass and the breviary again. At the visit's end Roncalli embraced the old man, invited him to a meal at the patriarchy and, as he left, slipped him some money.

Singing his patriarch's praises, this Don Giovanni treated everyone to drinks with the money. Criticized, Roncalli said quietly that he was not surprised at what had happened, but "it is a start to draw out the venom, if not from the blood, then from the soul."

Capovilla passed on to the patriarch advice not to give an appointment to a certain elderly individual. He was a member of Italy's Masonic movement, which at various times in the twentieth century had staged anti-Catholic demonstrations outside St. Peter's and been open about its desire to overthrow Catholicism. The appointment seeker might use a meeting for nefarious purposes, perhaps scandalizing Catholics by picturing Roncalli as in alliance with the Masons.

The cardinal "look[ed] at his counselor of human prudence," Capovilla recalled, and replied, "It would be... bad... for me to bar the door to anyone,...especially the aged."

So the elderly Mason came. There did not seem to be any aftereffects--for good or ill. However, sometime later, ill and "in need of light," as Capovilla put it, the Church's enemy turned to God and, among other things, sought the blessing of Roncalli, who was by this time pope.

Passing St. Mark's living quarters, a twenty-seven-year-old vacationing physician popped in an open door to "have a look around." With the gall of youth, he continued upstairs, where he encountered the cardinal patriarch, of whom he knew nothing. He was struck by "the [smiling] visage of a man who is good, simple and welcoming." Suddenly embarrassed, he explained his presence. With a graciousness that further mortified Doctor Felice Onofrio, Roncalli actually showed him around.

The doctor never forgot this encounter. Years later he would find himself, as one of the medical experts called in by the Congregation for the Causes of Saints, examining the cure eventually accepted as a miracle beyond medical explanation for John XXIII's beatification.

LIVING GOSPEL VALUES

The shepherd of everyone practiced pastoral outreach to *groups* too, in his usual ecumenical and sometimes daring fashion. It was an era when Catholics in general were scandalized and the shepherding Church condemnatory as—after the horrors of World War II—literature, film and art took radical turns toward the despairing and tawdry. During Roncalli's second year as cardinal patriarch, Venice hosted the Biennial Exhibit of Modern Art, routinely condemned by his predecessors. He did not like to go against former patriarchs but was open to the germs of goodness and truth in everything as well as everyone. That year he repeated the injunction that clergy not attend but in a nonhostile, nuanced way.

The next time, in 1956, he was ready for a radical change: He hosted a reception for all foreign and Italian delegations to the exhibition at his residence. As he chatted with his guests, they noted that the patriarch understood the themes of contemporary art. The following day Roncalli sent his own clerical delegate to the official opening. Several months later he himself visited the exhibition, as he would in 1958. Once again, as for centuries, the Church and art were brought together.

In October 1954 he represented the larger Church as pontifical legate at a Marian Congress in Lebanon. Afterward, sending a photo to one of two nun nieces, he commented that "persons with the fezzes on their heads are Moslems," adding that there was no need to omit the fact that among them were many "fine people."[10]

Around the elections of 1953, the Christian Democrats made overtures to the Socialists, who were moving away from their former Communist allies. The Vatican and most Venetian churchmen decried this "opening to the left" by the Christian Democrats. Three years later, in 1956, there was still great fear of a possible Communist-Socialist government. At this precise time Roncalli opened the doors of the Church to her proclaimed enemies. Completely upholding the line of the Vatican and his diocesan bishops, he forestalled a possibly more inflammatory Vatican intervention with a letter reminding Catholic voters, "It is an error to...be in league with an ideology, Marxism, which is a denial of Christianity."[11]

Yet his tone and style, while clearly differentiating gospel values from those of political ideologies that "suppress the inalienable rights of the human person and his or her immeasurable value,"[12] addressed Socialists, even Communists, as brothers whom time might bring home and who meanwhile had to be given respect both in regard to their free will and to their often honest, if misguided, intent to improve humanity's situation. As a biographer wrote, "Roncalli had a gift for finding the opportune moment and the right action...to create a more constructive" environment for dialogue and mutual respect.[13]

In February 1957 the National Congress of the Socialist Party was to be held in Venice. In anticipation, Roncalli sent a letter to the faithful, referring to the Socialists as "friends" and acknowledging appreciatively their desire to improve living conditions. In this nonadversarial tone he invited the Socialists to reconsider the Christian tradition they had repudiated, suggesting that they take note of spiritual realities and needs in addition to material ones.

He said he noted, with "at times very intense pain," that after twenty centuries of giving "life to... history, science, and art," religious truths were "dimmed, ignored, and neglected," and people believed they could "reconstruct the modern socioeconomic order on foundations other than Christ."

> Having spoken frankly,... as may be done among friends, I add my heartfelt wish that [the Venetian flock] would be welcoming and friendly, as is their custom. May they contribute to making worthwhile this gathering of so many brothers from different regions of Italy for a common elevation toward the ideals of truth, goodness, justice, and peace. And to this wish I add an invitation to those who believe, hope, and love, especially during this week, that heartfelt and pure prayers may be raised up to Almighty God for the benefit, consolation, and encouragement of all, so that they may understand, desire, and do what is good.[14]

Roncalli's eminently Christian letter resulted in a new, more positive attitude toward the Church by Italian Socialism. And farseeing individuals, such as the editor of *L'Osservatore Romano*, Count Giuseppe Della Torre, sent Roncalli private letters of praise. Yet even the Vatican newspaper, as well as Vatican radio, responded in ways that could be seen as repudiating this gospel approach to "enemies." Many northern Italian bishops were not pleased, nor were faithful who—under the pressure of legitimate fears of Communism—saw the world as "them" versus "us."

Told by Capovilla about the criticisms, Roncalli wrote in his diary February 26, 1957, "This was a source of pain for me, but not of humiliation. I am ready for anything. The moment for the 'science of humility' has arrived."[15]

"EMINENCE, DO YOU REALLY BELIEVE IN GOD?"

In Paris Roncalli had questioned whether he should be harsher. Now he was convinced that it was better to "sin" by too much love and mercy than by too much justice. "If the Eternal Father says to me, 'Roncalli, you needed to be harsher at times,' I will say, 'Eternal Father, it is You who sent Your Son to give me bad example.'"

Another of the myriad times he put this attitude into action was during the visit of a university professor and rector. The man told the Cardinal boldly, "I [only] want to speak about French literature with you; I'm not a believer."

"Willingly," was the serene reply. The two looked at books from the patriarch's library, chatting about the wonderful writings of the French. Then the visitor happened to refer to his mother's saying the rosary.

"Oh, do give my regards to your mother!"

This spontaneous, nonpolemic response cracked something, and the man who had wanted to stay strictly away from religion asked boldly, "Eminence, do you really believe in God?"

Roncalli continued to turn the leaves of the book he was showing the man. Finally he said gently, "Professor, I do not believe in God. I see God. I see God in your mother who says the little rosary. I see God in a little sick baby. Professor, with the prayers of your mother, one day you also will see God."

Not too long after, Roncalli became pope. As his university's rector, the professor sent best wishes.

Following Pope John's death, Capovilla again saw this professor, who asked, "Do you remember when I visited the pope when he was cardinal and we had that conversation?"

"Yes, I remember."

"Monsignor Capovilla, today I too see God."

CHRYSANTHEMUMS

The patriarch had four brothers. The one with whom his spirit had always most resonated was diagnosed with terminal cancer. Willingly offering his sufferings not just as prayer for his own wife and children but also for brother Angelo's ministerial needs, he died October 19, 1956.

This and other family deaths, the patriarch wrote a niece, assured that "my poor [cardinal's] purple is ornamented all over with chrysanthemums," the flowers traditionally placed on graves on All Souls' Day as symbols of death and, by extension, suffering and loss.[16] The years slowly emptying him of family satisfactions, Roncalli would have ample room one day soon to carry all humanity in that great heart.

But his thoughts were hardly so grandiose. As through his entire life, he made yearly retreats—in his Venice days with his clergy or with area bishops—but there was less need for spiritual retuning. In 1954, for the first time, he took no notes and instead wrote his will. Sure he had to be near the end of his life, his goal was to use his final days to "sanctify myself,"[17] making each day "one long prayer,"[18] detached from undue concern for exterior matters. He wrote, "[Every day] I try to do what the Lord wishes of me,... not worrying about tomorrow,... [just] doing what I can from hour to hour with great confidence and abandonment."[19]

On March 2, 1956, the greatly admired Pius XII celebrated his eightieth birthday and his seventeenth papal anniversary at a pontifical Mass in St. Peter's. Roncalli joined cardinals and bishops from every corner of the world, along with a crowd of fifty thousand, who were unaware of the fact that the pope was seriously ill.

In 1957 the patriarch reached road's end on his life's biggest literary undertaking. To be graced by a preface from Montini after Roncalli became pope, the work—begun in 1909 and published in five independent portions starting in 1936 as each part was completed—was collected in its final form into two volumes. Somewhat dry reading for non-scholars, the work compiled all the sixteenth-century records pertaining to a visitation of Saint Charles Borromeo to Bergamo. Not forgotten was the author's long-dead collaborator, who had rushed to comfort Roncalli when his father died. The opus is titled *The Acts of the Apostolic Visit of St Charles Borromeo to Bergamo (1575)*, edited by Angelo Giuseppe Roncalli with the collaboration of Don Pietro Forno.

That November he presided over the diocesan synod, having finished at last his parish visitations. He noted prophetically that the Church was ever young but still needed updating *(aggiornamento)*.

The year 1958 brought special events that pertained to former Venetian patriarch Saint Pius X, whose canonization Roncalli had attended in 1954. In March he traveled to Lourdes to consecrate a new underground church dedicated to the saint. That September he had celebrations in Venice for Saint Pius X's centennial of priestly ordination.

Earlier in the 1950s there were some prophecies from France, recalling the words of Queen Giovanna long ago, that Roncalli would also leave Venice to become pope. The patriarch dismissed them as "lunacy, lunacy"[20] and chose his Venice burial site.

On October 9, 1958, Pius XII died, and Cardinal Roncalli was off to Rome to help elect a successor.

❧ 12 ❧

Return to Rome

CARDINAL RONCALLI'S IMMEDIATE PRECONCLAVE LETTERS from Rome indicate two things: First, as he would solemnly attest later, he did nothing to bring about his election and would have been happy if found wanting; second, whether by human wisdom or that foreknowledge often found in the later stages of holiness, he was aware he was going to be elected the next pope.[1]

Not well known to the Church at large, Cardinal Roncalli's "cordiality," Capovilla pointed out, ensured he was a friend of many of the fifty-one other papal electors. Through his and other's travels, these included even people such as America's Cardinal Spellman.

After two long pontificates, what the majority wanted was a quiet regrouping period through a *transitional* pope. Good-natured, history-and-tradition-loving, seventy-seven-year-old Roncalli, by both temperament and age, would seem to ensure that. No one dreamed this holy and remarkable man would open the door to so many changes—some he favored and some he did not—in the papacy, the Church and even a world in peril of nuclear war.

Following one of the conclave voting sessions, Roncalli called for Monsignor Angelo Dell'Acqua, who had been his secretary his first five months in Istanbul and a friend ever after. Addressing him intimately as "Angelino mio," Roncalli solicited this younger friend: "I'm afraid some of these Cardinals want me to be the next pope. What do you believe I should do?"

Capovilla, who was present, heard Dell'Acqua reply: "Put it in the hands of God and don't be discouraged. Intelligent and generous collaborators won't be lacking."[2]

On October 28, 1958, Roncalli was elected.

The new pope would later comment that when he greeted the crowds for the first time immediately following his election, he felt all trussed up in a pinned-together white cassock hidden under a surplice. None of the three prepared sizes could accommodate his girth.

Capovilla recalled:

> He went to the balcony to give his blessing to the people in the piazza. He came back in and he greeted me. I knew that he had to prepare a [radio] message for the world for tomorrow and needed some help with this.
>
> I asked him, "Holy Father, do you want me to call someone?" He said, "My son, let me say vespers [and] compline [prayers] and my rosary in peace, and we'll talk about it later."
>
> This is equilibrium!

SINGING HIS PRAISES

Nevertheless in the new pope's diary on the day following his election, he noted that the whole world this day was speaking and writing of nothing "but me" and cried out for prayers to his mother, father, grandfather Angelo and great-uncle Zaverio, asking plaintively, "What did you do to deserve this honor?"[3]

Roncalli's friend, France's literary giant François Mauriac, spoke for many when he exclaimed that this pope would truly be a father.

If John retained serenity under the media blast, Capovilla pointed to a trait for which the new pope humbly thanked God in his journal some months later: "Above all, I am grateful to the Lord for the temperament he has given me.... I feel I am under obedience in all things, and... this... gives me... a strength of daring simplicity... [that] obtains universal respect and edifies many."[4]

He later defined *simplicity* as "love."[5] But it was more: love swathed in joyous gentleness and humble freedom from concern for any judgments but God's.

When he had first stepped onto the balcony of St. Peter's after the words *Habemus papam* boomed over the square, he had told the world that he would be called Giovanni XXIII, John XXIII. Why choose a name unused since the fifteenth century?

He gave a long explanation: "This name is sweet to me because it is the name of my father [Battista was *Giovanni* Battista] and it is delightful also because it is the title of the humble parish where I received baptism and [it is] the solemn name of innumerable cathedrals, spread over the entire world, firstly of the Sacred Lateran Basilica which is my cathedral [as Rome's bishop]."[6]

It was also, he went on, the name of two close to Jesus, his cousin John the Baptist and his beloved John the Evangelist, and, through the latter, a reminder that each of us is called to love.

In his first radio address the day following his election, he greeted the Church everywhere. He mentioned the unjust persecution she was suffering in the world's Communist sphere. Without condemning anyone, he expressed hope these sufferings would end through the conversion of governments.

More ecumenical than any pope before him, he quoted Jesus' desire that "they may all be one" (John 17:21) and declared that he wished to open heart and arms to the separated brethren.

The man who had helped so many dying young men in World War I and had sorrowed in World War II over murdered Jews, starving Greeks and "the lost" of all sides spoke of war's horrors. Neither chastising some nor exalting others, he told *all* the world's leaders to listen to their people. If they did, he said, they would hear cries for peace.

MORTIFICATIONS

There were a number of things about being pope that did not edify John XXIII. First was the sedan chair, which he termed "an exercise in mortification."[7] He noted this dislike at an audience but added that it reminded him of being carried on his father's shoulders, and we must let ourselves be carried by the Lord so as to carry him to others.

Following protocol, Capovilla at first genuflected to the pope and made a bow to the Eucharist. John was a man who loved traditions, but he eliminated that genuflection immediately: no more genuflections before one who, Christ's vicar or not, was just a man.

The first great function of John's papacy was the five-hour traditional coronation (today popes are "installed"), by his choice on November 4, feast of Saint Charles Borromeo. The ceremony tired John a little. Capovilla asked, "Are you pleased with the way things went?"

"How sad I was!" was the unexpected reply. "When I saw that poor old Cardinal Copello very unceremoniously told to take off his biretta and to kneel,... and then he incensed me on his knees three times as is done to the Eucharist. No, no, I prohibit this." Almost two years older than the pope, the longest-serving cardinal had been acting for them all.

Capovilla advised, "Let it go for now; [change things] slowly, slowly,"

"No, no, I don't want it!" John was adamant.

He had made one change already: During the coronation he addressed the people. Citing all the things a pope could be, he told them this "new pope is like the son of Jacob who, when he met his unfortunate brothers, laid bare... the tenderness of his heart, and bursting into tears, exclaimed: 'It is I,... your brother Joseph.'" As in Venice, he emphasized that he wanted to be for them an "image of the Good Shepherd."[8]

Another ceremony involved the fifty cardinals (one had died during the conclave), coming one by one to be received by the new pope. It took more than a day. Each made the traditional gesture of homage to him as Christ's representative (see Matthew 28:9), kissing first his feet and then his hand before being raised for a brotherly embrace.

At the end of the first day, the pope told Capovilla, "Tomorrow I don't want any of this foot kissing!" Capovilla tried to encourage him to let things stand for now, as dictated by long protocol based on a pope's "standing in" for Christ as King *and* from days when popes ruled the papal states. But John was again adamant: "I don't want this rite!" And nobody from that moment on was allowed to kiss his feet.

He also habitually forgot to use the papal *we* when he wrote anything out. Typists corrected him, and in public he read it as they had it. But when he talked to people, he always used *I*.

Prior Roger Schütz of Taizé, the great Protestant ecumenist, much later told John that Protestants were more scandalized by the Vatican's sumptuousness than they were by its doctrines. Sighed John, "Ah, pastor, look who you're talking to!" He added, "In my family we're poor. Don't you believe that I suffer [from these things]? But reform takes lots of time. You can't modify everything in a few years."[9]

Still, the changes he was able to make would endure.

To Business: The Big Scale

His first three messages—sent after his time of prayer on the evening of his election—were to the people of Venice, to Bergamo and to his family.

That same evening he summoned Cardinal Domenico Tardini, with whom he had been a seminarian decades before. Having served many years in the Curia, devout Domenico differed from John as greatly in experience as he did in temperament. He had been John's boss at times and, without malice, a hard taskmaster. John selflessly persuaded this incompatible person to fill the long-empty secretary of state position. Tardini, who had hoped to spend his last days at the orphanage he supported, had to give in. This appointment reassured the Curia and showed John's fearlessness toward collaborating with those who did not see the world as he did.

The new pope firmly believed that if Montini had been a cardinal, he would now be pope. Even before the coronation ceremonies, John had dashed off a letter by hand to Montini in Milan. He informed the archbishop to keep it quiet, but he was to be made a cardinal "right away."[10] Montini replied humbly that he read the letter on his knees.[11]

Other empty chairs in the College of Cardinals were filled. Usually listed in order of seniority, on *this* list Montini's name was first. John hesitated briefly when he added the twenty names that brought the college back to seventy, the number established in 1500 by Sixtus V. Then he reflected that the Church was in two-thirds more territory in 1958 than in 1500, and he named three more cardinals, among them his worthy Bergamo seminary colleague Gustavo Testa, at the time nuncio in Switzerland.

He also broke another tradition that anyone with a blood brother in the College could not be named when he picked long-time nuncio to the United States Gaetano Cicognani (who would replace Tardini as secretary of state when Tardini died in July 1961 of a massive heart attack).

Also among the twenty-three was Richard Cushing, archbishop of Boston. The pope told Capovilla that Cushing was neither theologian nor biblicist and knew almost nothing of Latin, but "he is a pastor and he has a great big heart—which is very important!"

With these appointments and others in 1959, 1960, 1961 and 1962, John would add fifty-two cardinals. He internationalized the college by appointing the first Japanese, Filipino and African cardinals and cutting back on Italians, so that for the first time they were no longer the majority.

At last he had a chance to use some of his insights from Bulgaria, particularly the one about problems arising when people in Rome made decisions for those far away. Naming over a thousand bishops, he tried, outside Europe, to select locals whenever possible. *Prince of Shepherds*, one of his eight encyclicals, promoted creating local hierarchies and fostering native vocations. Especially in Asia and Africa, he recommended that these vocations be formed in seminaries run by their own people. His goal: to transform as quickly as possible mission churches run by European clergy into local churches run by native clergy. The one-time Catholic Action associate also gave prominence to the laity's importance in bringing their countries to Christ.

The new pope's concerns included the Church diplomats who represent Catholicism around the world and have so much power to make the Church enemies or friends. The Turks demonstrated the latter vividly when, in 1959, the Islamic nation sent first its external affairs minister and then its president to congratulate its former nonaccredited apostolic delegate. Another example: the friendly goodwill of Greek Orthodox Ecumenical Patriarch Athenagoras, based on Roncalli's long-before dealings with Greek and Turkish Orthodox.

By June 1959 John had summoned now Archbishop Giacomo Testa—intimate friend and kindred soul—who had been in the pope's old Turkey-Greece post since John went to Venice. John made him president of the Pontifical Academia Ecclesiastica, the Church's school for its diplomats. Recalling Radini Tedeschi, Pope John would be responsible for a complete renovation of the academy's physical interior, even as he trusted Giacomo to form the men inside. The aim, as the new pope had written long ago of Radini Tedeschi: to be builders of souls.

OPENING HEART AND ARMS TO THE EASTERN CHURCHES

Besides his important responsibility forming diplomats, the once slim, now round, genial Testa was appointed both a consultor of the Sacred Congregation for Religious and a consultor of the Sacred Congregation for the Oriental Church.[12] Some saw him as John's eyes and ears, but to the pope, Giacomo carried to both groups a spirit twin to John's in love and understanding, particularly toward the Eastern Churches.

In 1960 Giacomo would add his many years of experience in Catholic-Orthodox relations to a commission of mostly Pontifical Oriental Institute professors doing preparatory work in this area for the Vatican Council. He would direct a subcommission studying non-Catholic Oriental churches with John's deep respect for Orthodoxy.

To further help the non-Latin rites, several years later, in August 1962, John appointed *Gustavo* Testa secretary of the Sacred Congregation for the Oriental Churches. Gustavo had spent almost twenty years in Eastern rite territories before the Switzerland posting. And he shared the open heart and arms of John and Giacomo.

THE SMALL SCALE: BISHOP OF ROME

Back in 1958, shortly after the new pope's radio call to unity, he had made another ecumenical gesture. Heading to St. John Lateran on Sunday, November 23, to be installed as Rome's bishop, he stopped at St. Clement's Church to honor Eastern Catholics and the Orthodox by praying at the tombs of the great Slavic brother evangelizers, Saints Cyril and Methodius. (The Iron Curtain would not let him, even as pope, give Slavic Bulgaria a seminary, but second best, a Slavic College would arise in Rome.)

John's diary noted "one of the most beautiful days of my life," describing his formal entry into his Cathedral of St. John Lateran as Rome's bishop and "the simply triumphant" return to St. Peter's, with a "touching and unexpected, and for this reason much more dear" homage from crowds of Romans lining the route while the two cardinals with him wept with emotion.[13]

The journal entry continues: "I could only hold myself in humiliation, as a sacrificial offering for my people, but in great and joyful simplicity."

Unlike some previous popes, Pope John *acted* as a new diocesan bishop, making pastoral visits and important gestures. One of the first was a visit to the diocesan seminary. Abandoning the expected formal statement, he delighted the seminarians by spontaneously dialoguing about friendship and confidence.

He confided to them that he found himself thinking, "I must refer this to the pope," or, "I must report that to the pope," then suddenly remembered *he* was the pope. He described the purpose of his new ministry: "to be the servant of the servants of God—unworthily but because the Lord has wished it," emphasizing, "He, not I, not I!"

He shared that every time he was called "Holiness," he felt confusion and embarrassment. Comfortably making them his equal by calling them "you…my friends," he begged they ask God to grant him the holiness his title imputed. A pope has no value for the Church and souls, he added solemnly, if he is not holy in fact as well as name.[14]

He continued this informal touch, opening the academic year at the papal university, the Lateran Atheneum. To the expected formal address, he added his memories of teaching there just before being sent to Bulgaria.

On December 22 he showed his regard for Rome's diocesan priests by having all 170 as guests at the Vatican. Every year thereafter, as Lent began, he met with his pastors, always offering recommendations for fruitful preaching. These included:

- prepare seriously with study and *prayer*;
- keep it simple—aimed at a precise goal;
- touch the heart to change lives;
- be sure to teach *all* the basic truths of the faith;
- aim for the best praise of all, that your listeners find in you a true image "of the good Jesus."[15]

Over his five lenten seasons, he visited twenty-five parishes and participated four times in diocesan Ash Wednesday penitential processions. Responding to need, he soon sought out parishes in areas where poor, often ignorant people eked out a living and were hostile or oblivious to the Church. These people turned out in immense crowds and, in one often reported instance, took down their political banners during a fierce election to replace them with homemade signs welcoming "the Good Pope." Some saw in this humanity's innate spiritual hunger for the God of tender mercies John represented so well.

In January 1960 he opened the first diocesan synod Rome had had since 1725, its second since 1461. This synod— for a city grown from four hundred thousand inhabitants in 1900, a year before he began his studies there, to a sprawling, often unrooted two million—would be a junior version of the coming summons of the whole Church to council.

There are those who criticized even having a diocesan synod. He brought them into the process. And after the synod he said to those still unsatisfied that the next could be better, no doubt, but he had made this beginning, imperfect or no.

SMALLER STILL

The pope also had governance of the little "nation," the Vatican state. Pope Pius's years of illness had led to neglect, from the shrunken College of Cardinals down to insufficient wages for Vatican workers. By talking, as he always did, to these folks too, John discovered things were not as they should be. The son of the peasant sharecropper moved immediately to see that wages were brought up to standard. The most lowly paid found a 36 percent increase in their pockets, the highest earners 12 percent. He also set up family allowances and pension benefits.

SMALLEST OF ALL

Smallest of all was the pope's household. Within the papal apartment above St. Peter's Square, there was what one could almost call a coziness that belied whose residence it was. This was not due to that lifelong impulse to concern himself with the material aspects of the places he lived: In his room, for instance, the furniture of Pius XII remained, even many of the man's books still on the shelves. If John had made the papal bedroom "his," it was only with lots of religious art, along with a multitude of framed photos of beloved family members, friends and those priest benefactors who had helped form his soul and aspirations. The hominess was rooted in John's nature, a pope who--dignified in office but devoid of any pretensions of superiority as a person—chatted familiarly with those who worked there and couldn't picture himself dining alone as a silent server glided in and out.

Above all the atmosphere could be pinpointed to John's choice of living companions. He had brought with him not just Capovilla, a man who loved simplicity as he did, but also the former fishing village resident Guido Gusso and those humble women, his friends and Venice housekeepers, Bergamo's Sisters of the Poor. A trio of sisters occupied the housekeepers' quarters in the papal apartment. They became a quartet in August 1962, when it was felt wise to add a nurse to the household.

Rounding out the group, since more hands were needed to keep a papal bark afloat than a patriarchal one, was Guido's brother Giampaolo. The brothers drove him (but not, with Roncallian charity, until Pius's chauffeur had died), served at table and handled valet functions, such as keeping track of and helping John into the proper garments for a pope's varied functions.

Denying himself having any of his relatives live with him, even his nun nieces or priest nephew, his father's heart, as it had in Paris and Venice, continued to form all who *did* live with him into something beyond a household. Asked to describe it, one of the sisters, mentioning the morning Mass John said for them all, the pre-supper rosary together and John's interest in their families, could only repeat several times, "It was like a family."[16]

CHRISTMAS 1958

John's way of celebrating his first papal Christmas two months after his election surprised the world and was widely reported by an approving press. Suddenly the new Roman pontiff was a father figure far beyond his apartment. And the way the world in general thought about popes, and even in many cases the Church, changed.

His Midnight Mass had been, as traditional, for the diplomatic corps, representing all the world's peoples. Christmas morning he celebrated two more Masses and gave the traditional greeting and blessing *Urbi et Orbi* ("To the City and the World").

After that the papal Christmas seemed all new. Instead of settling down for a well-deserved rest, the seventy-eight-year-old pope rode over to the Vatican children's hospital, Bambini Jesu, walking from room to room to visit children stricken with polio. Then he went on to Holy Spirit Hospital, visiting adults bedside to bedside there too, once he got past a hastily formed line of welcoming dignitaries. Quipping that he saw nothing in Scripture that said the pope must eat alone, he had changed that "rule" right away. For Christmas lunch he invited Don Loris Capovilla, whom he had just made a monsignor (and who, the pope noted, sported his new garb for the first time), and retired eighty-five-year-old Archbishop Angelo Rotta, a friend of forty years who was his predecessor in Turkey and collaborator, as nuncio there, in rescuing Jews in Hungary.

That afternoon, Capovilla recalls, John did more entertaining. The pope's secretary mentions two groups of handicapped people from homes run by priests and the boy singers of the Sistine Chapel choir. (It is possible, as other sources mention, that boys from the orphanage maintained by Cardinal Tardini were there too).

The next day John visited the prisoners at Rome's *Regina Coeli* prison. By now the press, and those who seek importance by association, were out in force. In his diary the pope noted, "I was hemmed in on all sides: authorities, photographers, prisoners, warders –but the Lord was close." He continued that exercising the works of mercy was among the consolations of a pope, expressing surprise that so much was being made of this visit, "such a simple and natural thing for me."[17] In fact, the place was awash with tears from those for whom it was anything but natural to be visited by a pope of any kind, let alone a loving, fatherly one who told them salvation was for them too and chatted about his own relative once jailed for poaching.

PERSONAL MATTERS
Having gotten hold of a typewriter, in December 1961 he sent his family, via its head, his one-year-younger brother, a letter.

He warned about those who would exploit family members for financial gain. But mainly he expressed his pleasure that the Roncalli name was known with approval and respect worldwide.

He knew that some family members had suffered mortifications from being related to a pope, especially one who let his family remain in their social condition—it had been suggested to John, among other things, that he make his brothers counts—but he wrote: "The honor of a pope is [gained] not from enriching his relatives but only from assisting them with charity according to their needs and each one's condition," and, "This sacrifice I impose on myself in regard to you does more honor to me and to you, [and] gains more respect and sympathy than you could possibly believe or imagine."[18]

In regard to the papal girth, Capovilla said that John "ate with appetite and pleasure, but modestly." But after a lifetime of no chance for regular exercise, often eating on the run, years of lavish diplomatic meals and probably stress-eating, John was fat.

Still, as he turned eighty, his stamina was remarkable. Capovilla said, "For example, if he was tired, he went to bed at nine. Then he might get up at 11 and work until 2 or 3, then go back to sleep for a couple of hours." If during the day Capovilla found John looking "fatigued," the secretary recalled that arranging for the pope to have fifteen minutes of rest and perhaps a cup of broth or milk was all it took for John to be ready to go again.

It was an era when diets were suspected of ruining health. Instead John's doctors gave him medication to induce weight loss. He didn't complain, but the sisters saw the stuff was so vile that it brought tears to his eyes and they stopped it.

At last he began getting regular exercise, afternoon walks in the Vatican gardens. One official decided to end tourists' access to the heights of St. Peter's, because from there the strolling pope could be seen. John squashed this, chuckling, "But why can't the faithful look? I don't do anything that would give cause for scandal."[19]

That certainly was true. Capovilla remembered seeing John frequently lost in prayer during visits to a replica of the Lourdes grotto.[20]

Prayer may not subtract pounds, but it too is a health-benefiting exercise.

❧ 13 ❧

A Fatherly Holy Father

JOHN XXIII WAS THE ONLY POPE TO DATE TO HAVE PASSED decades in non-Catholic, non-Christian and rapidly de-Christianizing nations and cultures, the only one to actually live among and collaborate on humanitarian endeavors with Eastern rite Catholics, Orthodox Christians and Muslims. As far back as World War I, he had put himself at the service of varied Protestants, while during World War II he had worked hand in hand with Jews. Strongly secular milieus, such as postwar Paris, were also familiar territory where his warmth and goodness had made him many nonreligious admirers and even friends.

He had interacted successfully with members, even leaders, of groups who feared or hated the Church. His personal friendships included Socialists, agnostics and others who were feared and sometimes hated by most "exemplary"

Christians. Capovilla quoted the atheist-turned-Catholic Madeleine Delbrêl: "After his first few weeks as pope, many of us began to realize how evangelically illiterate we were."[1]

Catholic writer Henri Fesquet claimed that John "put himself on an equal footing with the people by his disdain for honors,...aversion to luxury...[and] exquisite cordiality." And Fesquet repeated a Communist worker's comment: "'There's a man I'd gladly sit down to have a drink with!'"[2]

John would have smiled. To all humans in their varied guises of faith or nonfaith, it was "the good pope's" style to offer goodwill and respect.

Toward Unity

God had laid a burden of working for unity on John's heart. It helped in that regard that his natural inclination was to stress what united rather than what separated Catholics and non-Catholics.

He had also early mastered distinguishing between a theological position and the person holding the position. A position might be worthless; each person, made in God's image, was of inestimable value.

Another plus: In his first encounters with non-Catholics, during World War I, he had determined, when meeting them, to speak the truth with love. He never watered down what he and the Church believed. At the same time, those he spoke to were the objects of a love that wished good to all. The fruit: Over the years, as he collaborated with people of other faiths to help the suffering, there was neither confusion about what each stood for nor wrangling over beliefs.

ANGLICANS

Anglicans and Orthodox, to John, were "our separated brothers" —baptized Christians after all, although some Catholic authorities in the 1960s were loath to acknowledge that or any point of unity. And he acted toward them in brotherly fashion. With the support of a German Cardinal named Augustin Bea—and almost no one else— John received the archbishop of Canterbury and head of the Anglican communion, Dr. Geoffrey Fisher, in December 1960.

Capovilla recalled that the prospective visit met with such disapproval it was kept under wraps, with only Capovilla to greet the archbishop and lead him to the pope. There was not a word in the news about what Capovilla pointed out was an historic occasion: An archbishop of Canterbury and a pope had not met since the Reformation four hundred years earlier.

John's warmth triumphed over the Catholic opposition's snub. Although Fisher retired immediately after, the next Anglican archbishop of Canterbury, joined by the Anglican archbishop of York, appointed an official representative to the Vatican. He too was received by John, on July 12, 1961.

Capovilla also related an incident regarding the last days in 1960 of England's ambassador to the Vatican, Anglican Sir Marcus Cheke, "a good and practicing Christian":

> One morning the pope received a note from the secretary of state alerting him that this diplomat was dying. John was asked if he would like to send a message expressing his good wishes.
>
> "Send a message? Wouldn't it be better for me to go?"

The response to the pope was that such a thing was unheard of. But go John did, not with fanfare but making a simple, quiet visit [to a private clinic], with just myself accompanying him.

The two of us were in the room with the ambassador and his wife. On the table lay a crucifix and a Bible.

Ever the diplomat, the ambassador first said, "Holy Father, I thank you for the honor you give to England." Then he added that he and his wife were offering the sacrifice of his life "for the union of Christians."

Pope John was very touched by these words.

"Ambassador, you know whom I represent.... Would you permit me that we pray together?"

Catholics and Protestants praying together in this period was not acceptable practice, but the pope and the diplomatic couple prayed the Our Father together anyway. Then John picked up the crucifix and offered it to the ambassador and his wife to kiss. Before leaving, he embraced each and said, "We'll see each other again"— not the standard view the faiths had then of each other's eternity.

The pope went home very content and moved emotionally. He said he hoped he didn't scandalize anyone by his prayer.

"No, no," I assured him before John retired.

Not long after that an illustrious person greeted me. His query: "Did the person convert?"

I replied boldly: "Your Excellency, this act was not about conversion but charity."

JEWS

In spite of Israel's being one of the nations, like Turkey, with whom there existed no official diplomatic relations, John made the friendly gesture of having his election communicated by the Vatican to the Jewish state. In response: a telegraphed blessing from Israel's chief rabbi Isaac Herzog, who had traveled to Turkey years earlier to thank John for wartime aid to Jews.

The worldwide Jewish community appreciated even more the pope's order, his first papal Easter season, that the phrase "the perfidious Jews" be dropped from the Church's Good Friday prayers. Originally meaning "without faith," the word *perfidious* had evolved into "faithless" in the sense of terrible betrayal and unthinkable treachery.

An encouraged French Jewish scholar—whose family had died in the Holocaust—got an audience with the pope. Doctor Jules Isaac pointed out that anti-Semitism was fostered by the belief of many Catholics that all Jews were forever cursed, having "killed Christ." Holders of this pernicious view cited Scripture: "His blood be on us and on our children!" (Matthew 27:25)

Having seen up close the horrors anti-Semitism can unleash, John listened with great sympathy. He had already taken steps toward Jewish-Catholic dialogue that would bring about historic changes. Emphasized today is Church teaching that the sins of *everyone* led Jesus to the cross and that, no hapless victim, he offered himself freely in sacrificial atonement for all.

John's diary also notes a visit from 130 to 140 Jews, whom Capovilla identified as American members of the Jewish

Study Mission under Rabbi Herbert Friedman. Widely reported was the pope's referring to his relationship to them, reflecting his middle name, Giuseppe, with the touching biblical words, "It is I, Joseph your brother." In turn, Rabbi Friedman expressed gratitude for John's work on behalf of Jews fleeing Hitler. This led John to share with them his memory of helping divert the boatload of Jewish children from an enemy port in those days.

It was for such successful rescues, and other attempted ones, that Rabbi Herzog had traveled to Istanbul to thank Archbishop Roncalli. John told his visitors that the rabbi and he had experienced "a meeting of hearts" and "human brotherhood."[3]

PROTESTANTS

Belgian Cardinal Leon Suenens, in his autobiography, *Memories and Hopes*, told of bringing to the Vatican a Methodist couple and asking John if he would see the pair. As Suenens led them in, he was taken aback to see the pope scurrying around, rearranging chairs in order to make his guests comfortable. The couple couldn't thank Suenens enough for making this visit possible.[4]

Capovilla mentioned another Methodist who left an audience quoting John's beloved, read and reread—and very Catholic—spiritual guide, *The Imitation of Christ* by Thomas à Kempis.

FRIENDS FOREVER

John said, and meant, that he himself was nothing. But paradoxically (students of sanctity will understand this), that in no way precluded healthy self-esteem. He remained comfortable with himself and comfortable with others. Even in old age—due to his goodness, Capovilla said—John had the rare ability of making new friends. Yet, Capovilla stressed, no friend took a place away from another. Even as pope, John neither dropped old friends nor changed toward them.

Guglielmo Carozzi, an important figure among the priests of the Bergamo diocese, had been a seminarian in Bergamo and in Rome with the pope. They had been friends almost seventy years, and genial Carozzi wanted to see his old companion. Ushered by Capovilla into the private papal rooms, Carozzi immediately dropped to his knees, trying to kiss John's feet.

He was stopped with a shocked, "Don Gelmo, what are you doing? I'm the same as those long ago years." And then to remind him who it really was before him, John added, "Remember our good Mamas [coming] on visiting days at the seminary?"[5]

A similar situation occurred when the nine-years-older Cardinal Georges Grente of Le Mans, France, visited. Because they were old friends, he forgot to call John "Your Holiness," and began to weep over the mistake.

John immediately assured him that he, John, *wasn't* holy, and the title was unimportant. "What's important is our friendship."[6]

He had younger friends too. Don Andrea Spada, twenty-seven years John's junior, was editor of the Bergamo diocesan paper for which then Don Roncalli often wrote. As Spada entered the room for a visit with the pope, a cannon fired, announcing noon. The pope reminded his guest that in Bergamo this was when the *polenta* was put on the table and people recited the Angelus. "If you like, we could recite it now," he offered. And they did.[7]

In October 1960, two years after John became pope, someone informed him that a priest with whom he had been in school in 1894 was ill. This Don Giovanni Filippi, pastor of a parish, received a loving letter from John, assuring him that they were always good companions and "brothers."[8]

And in January 1961 the pope wrote a tender letter by hand to the ailing Monsignor Giovanni Dieci. Long ago John had handpicked Dieci and brought him from Bergamo to Rome to serve as secretary in the missions office from 1920 to 1925. Now John assured this ever dear friend that the pope suffered with him and asked Dieci to unite *his* sufferings to his old friend's for the work of Christ and the Church.[9]

Dozens of similar kindnesses kept flames of friendship bright.

SIMPLY HIMSELF

When John, as pope, appeared at public audiences, he tried to follow the instructions he was given about how to enter, how to exit and all the other protocol points. But he was no stickler. Once, having had some mistake brought to his attention for a third or fourth time, he said, "I'm a novice; little by little, I'll improve."[10]

He remained himself publicly too, using ordinary words and tones. During a large public audience he was talking amid the clustered entourage, a prelate on either side of him, a major domo and a chamberlain, plus hovering secret service men. A baby's cry drowned him out, and the pope, who had passed his childhood amid the din of twenty children, and infants said very naturally to Monsignor Callori di Vignale on his right, "Go see what's going on with this poor baby." Mortally embarrassed, the celibate monsignor approached an equally mortified mother. The infant looked at the stranger, and the wails ceased. Perhaps a prayer from John?[11]

He never tried to seem to know more than he did. Thus he told a group of German pilgrims in German how sorry he was that he couldn't tell them of his esteem for their country. Cologne's Archbishop Josef Frings interrupted to say that John spoke German very well. Chuckling, John replied that those words plus the phrase that he didn't speak German made up his entire knowledge of the language.[12]

Capovilla recalled that when John was recording a message to the world for radio broadcast, he coughed.

"We'll have to redo it," he was told.

"But why? It's natural to cough."

A letter prepared for a cardinal would be presented to the pope in Gothic type and addressed very formally, such as Venerable Father. The pope would lament, "But we were in the seminary together," and add above the title, "and most beloved brother." When told, "Now we have to write it again," he would insist, "But no, this is a sign of our humanity. Now he will say, 'The Holy Father actually did this document and made it his own.'"

Capovilla also remembered letters being prepared for someone celebrating fifty years of priesthood or forty years as a bishop. Naturally, John could not write this huge number of letters himself. But he would look at some of these and say, "This is a cold letter. It could be sent to anyone. I've had personal relations with him. I know him. He has to see that it comes from my heart, not from the pen of another." And changes would be made.

A BLUNDER

Holiness and abounding goodwill, insisted Capovilla, did not "erase human limitations, natural defects, flaws of upbringing."[13] In short, even saints aren't perfect. In that vein, the pope's secretary recalled June 8, 1960, when the very devout thirty-year-old King Badouin of Belgium and his wife Fabiola had an audience with John. King Badouin told John that the queen wanted to share first with the pope that they were expecting a baby. The pope, who felt life had no riches to compare with God's gift of a child, was moved and said, "What a great grace God is giving you." Both of them knelt, but before the pope could bless them, Fabiola raised her eyes and said, "Your Holiness, we are not expecting a successor to the throne; we are expecting a saint."

This extraordinary couple—since Badouin's death in 1993 he has been proposed for sainthood—left John so touched that, without thinking, he mentioned the coming birth to journalists, who always hover when a pope receives people of importance. This was a sad blunder, for the child was miscarried. Fabiola and Badouin would give the world examples of sanctity but never a child.

AN INNOCENT CHILD AND SOME SINNERS

A woman and her little girl arrived from the United States. Dying from leukemia—untreatable at the time—little Katherine wanted to see Rome and, once there, Pope John. A reporter somehow heard about this and published a brief anecdote.

Thus John learned of the child. He immediately granted a private audience with the proviso that no journalists be present. While a pope must let his good deeds shine, this one was not about to make "good press" from a dying child.

After a visit with the mother, through an interpreter John had a long conversation alone with the child. What was said is private. But a photo attests that this was no "story," because John permitted the papal photographer in when all was over, to give the family a souvenir of the meeting.[14]

It happened from time to time that Catholic clergy erred or even sinned gravely and had to be removed from their posts or disciplined. Capovilla recalled the great humility—not weakness—in John that insisted the truth be told, but always with goodness and love. For instance, when the writings of a priest had to be disclaimed because they contradicted the truths of the faith, John was vigilant that the errors were clearly stated but that their author was not attacked.

"John said in such instances, 'Yes, we have to do this, to "make the provision" [literally, to discipline], but remember what Jesus did with Peter, who denied him. If it had been we, we wouldn't have accepted him back anymore.'"

John's goal was to emulate Christ. And like Christ, he knew humanity. So when John "had to remove a bishop or a priest, he didn't rip his clothes nor was he surprised; he said, 'Poor creature, see what happened to him. God has been very good to me. He had his hand on my head,'" implying that without grace he could have done the same.

One day a bishop John had to remove from office came to Rome seeking an audience. Vatican officials would have said no, so the man sagely sent a letter to papal secretary

Capovilla. He wrote humbly that he was a sinner and wanted to personally ask pardon of the pope. Capovilla showed the letter to John, who responded, "Let him come."

"John received the man as a brother, showed him respect by calling him by his title and said, 'Your Eminence, let's not talk about that thing [the malfeasance that had stripped him of his position]. I have arranged for you to be in a monastery treated with respect and honor.'"

John ended the interview saying humbly, "Let's pray together to the Lord."

Capovilla said that in his holiness "John was [as clear as] a drop of water, his soul as innocent as a baby." Therefore egotism and sin made him very sad, while his view of mankind—each made in the image of God—gave him equal pleasure in speaking to John Eisenhower ("We share the same name!" he exclaimed happily.), son of the U.S. president, or in speaking to the Eisenhowers' driver when they visited the pope on December 6, 1959.

Another Capovilla anecdote:

In the time of Pius XII, there was a noble, princely family that had a job in the Vatican. The young prince was one of the *dolce vita,* that is, a group of aristocrats and artists who, around 1960, were living in debauchery, without respect for themselves, God or others. Pius suspended the prince from his post.

After Pius died, the young man went to the secretary of state, wanting to be reinstated even though he had not changed his life. Brazenly, he sought an audience with John. The secretary of state was against it, but John received the young man respectfully and heard him out before saying that if his predecessor had taken this action, John must respect it. Undeterred, the prince kept insisting his former honorific Vatican title be reestablished.

Tired and already ill at the time, John ended the audience. It was 2 pm and the last audience of the day.

The butler came to accompany John from the reception room to his apartment. In the elevator John asked, "Guido, your father was a fisherman, right?"

"No, Holy Father, my uncle was the fisherman, my father was a baker."

"Oh. You know, your father was a baker, your uncle a fisherman, my father a farmer; we are more noble— we—than the person who just left us."

CONFLICTS IN THE CHURCH AND A PATIENT POPE

For the seventieth anniversary of Pope Leo XIII's landmark encyclical *Rerum Novarum* ("Of New Things"), which had spoken out on behalf of the working class and social justice, John issued the encyclical *Mater et Magistra* ("Mother and Teacher") in May 1961, to update Catholic social teaching. While stressing the importance of Catholics' adhering to Church social doctrine, the encyclical took into account the fact that, following the horrors of World War II, *within* the Church there were "upright and sincere Catholics" with dramatically differing views on how to *apply* Catholic doctrine to concrete economic and political situations.[15] John respected that diversity but cited the duty to search for as much convergence as possible through respectful discussion. He longed to foster within the Church mutual consideration and reciprocal respect. He suffered when disagreeing parties violated Christ's call to charity.

John's own practice of charity toward those who opposed him had always been heroic and did not cease now that he was pope. A striking example was his comment in sweet tones to a well-known cardinal who, no doubt with well-meaning fervor, often worked against the pope rather than supporting him. "Eminence," the pope said, "our two heads are a little far apart, but our hearts are close together."

Because of John's quarter century of active historical research, he always saw present matters against the long panorama of the Church's past. This kept him from quick judgments in several controversies.

On worker-priests, for instance, he understood that there was much to be said on the side of upholding priestly dignity and avoiding temptations that might lead priests to be unchaste or become Communist. There was also much to be said for taking the Church to a working class that too often found it irrelevant or despised it. One of the congregations suspended this initiative, and John upheld the suspension, but as a temporary solution to be ratified or rectified at Vatican II.

On the application of new methods of studying the Bible, promoted by Pius XII, he saw too the praiseworthy effort to advance knowledge. But he did not overlook the worries of other churchmen that rationalistic, materialistic analysis could produce scholars who turned away from the Fathers and the Magisterium to deny the supernatural, including even Christ's miracles.[16] The sides were already warring, and not very charitably.

He took some action, letting it be clear that what *he* wanted was "a biblical [institution and attitude]...of such depth and dignity...as to become a point of reference and esteem for all our separated brethren who, when they abandoned the Catholic Church, took refuge as an escape and salvation in the shadow of the Sacred Book, differently read and interpreted."[17]

But on both issues—worker-priests and Bible study methods—John's principle was to not make strong decisions based on his own ideas but to patiently let opposing forces grapple until the Spirit should make clear the right course. He would die before either of these particular issues was resolved.

John did immediately make efforts, sadly ignored by some, to stop churchmen from meddling in Italy's politics. Not that he thought the Church should refrain from weighing in on issues. But he wanted this done by educating the faithful, so that they would arrive at their voting decisions with an informed conscience. He had done this in Venice, in his letter that stated clearly how Christian and Socialist values differed.[18]

❦ 14 ❦

The Council

THERE ARE MANY ANECDOTES ABOUT THE PRECISE MOMENT when Pope John XXIII decided to hold a churchwide ecumenical council— "ecumenical" in the sense of worldwide and universal, not in that of today's common usage of bringing together faiths. His great-nephew Marco Roncalli, in a 2006 interview, quoted the pope's saying the idea did not come "as the fruit of a prolonged meditation but as the spontaneous flower of an unexpected spring" conceived in prayer, thus to be accepted as a divine inspiration from God.[1]

That in no way negates the fact, insisted Marco Roncalli, that as far back as his service in Istanbul, his great-uncle had spoken about a council to Marco's father and others. Many, including popes, had talked about a council. In this pope's case, at least as early as the Modernism crisis under Pius X, he had been ruminating on how to bring the Church to people in a changing human society.

Once the inspiration came to him as pope, he spoke about what was on his mind to many. Augustinian bishop Peter Canisius Van Lierde reported that John confided, "I'm going to announce a Vatican Council. It's a divine inspiration."[2] Others reported similar statements.

PREPARATIONS

John, typically, wanted everyone to have a say, although he made it clear that the Church was not meeting to promulgate new doctrines. Emphasis was to be on the pastoral, not the doctrinal. In other words, *how* to teach, not *what* to teach. Questionnaires went to bishops, general superiors of orders, university leaders and others. What did they think needed discussing?

That John was truly open is shown in his attitude toward the huge number of requests to discuss changing the liturgy's Latin into the vernacular. He himself had tried—and failed— to introduce a little vernacular when serving in countries where most Catholics, usually foreign, looked down on the native language. But not into the Mass proper. For instance, in Istanbul, in 1936, he had introduced the recital in Turkish of the Divine Praises at Benediction services.

Letters to two seminarian nephews before he became pope show a deep love for Latin. John not only was familiar with Latin works; he loved them in a personal not just a scholarly way. Besides using phrases from the language frequently in his official and personal writings, as pope, he was reading for enjoyment and profit—in its original Latin—an ancient papal predecessor. Yet, setting his feelings aside, he accepted these requests for use of the vernacular as "serious and worthy of respect."[3]

The pope knew from his years among fearful, suspicious Orthodox that no council could affect reunion at this time. Still, John would lay groundwork toward Christian unity in the limited ways possible among equally fearful and suspicious Catholic leaders, who shrank from even his—to him—simple gesture of receiving the archbishop of Canterbury.

Only three months into his papacy, he decreed that the "faithful of the separated Churches" be invited to participate as observers in the coming council. Early in 1962 he sent Archbishop Giacomo Testa and another churchman to Greek Orthodox Patriarch Athenagoras. They briefed Athenagoras on the council, expressing John's regard for this brother in Christ and issuing the pope's personal invitation that Greek Orthodoxy participate. The Greek patriarch longed to send observers but couldn't due to inner Orthodox turmoil. But John's invitation bore future fruit in a meeting of Paul VI and the patriarch. The decision of many other Christian churches to send observers changed Catholic-Protestant relations forever.

AN ECUMENICAL COLLABORATOR

A lifelong friend wrote that John "was born with an ecumenical mind,"[4] but in his era not a lot of others—of any faith—shared that trait. Spirit-inspired, he was certain, to work toward Christ's flock being one again, John found a collaborator unexpectedly in a man he met only after becoming pope.

Born the same year as John, German Jesuit Augustin Bea had been Pius XII's confessor and a consultor for the Holy Office, which handled any potential ecumenical activities. He shared John's desires to promote Christian unity and repudiate anti-Semitism. Capovilla said the learned Bea became one of John's "soul friends," and Bea said John and he "understood one another perfectly," adding, "My personal contacts with Pope John were always a deeply personal and joyful spiritual feast of the spirit for me."[5]

John looked to Bea for initiatives that would forever change for the better Catholic-Jewish relations. The pope also entrusted Bea with a new institution asked for by a European bishop, the Secretariat for Christian Unity. Formed to facilitate contacts with other Christians, under Bea this secretariat extended those invitations John wanted to Protestant groups to send observers to the council.

The invitations led to an event that was the summit of John XXIII's lifelong efforts to promote unity among Christians. Two days after the council opened on October 13, 1962, forty observers representing almost every one of the great Christian confessions, including many Eastern Churches, came to visit the pope.

Before they arrived John entered the room where these guests were to be received and saw that an elevated throne had been prepared for him. "Bring that chair down," he immediately ordered. He knew, explained Capovilla, that this seating arrangement would be offensive in a situation that called for being a brother with brothers. Thus the chairs were arranged in an oval, the pope's chair only minimally elevated.

John did not talk about dogma or theology with his guests—all knew their differences. Instead he reminisced about his contacts with other Christians over the years and the deep friendships he had made, relationships filled with mutual respect and appreciation. He asked them to read his heart to see the brotherly love there. And he spoke of his anxiety for unity, ending that this longing "[inspires] me to tell you of the resolve burning in my soul to work and suffer so that the hour will come when the prayer of Jesus at the Last Supper will be accomplished."

Historic enemies heard the Catholic pope with tear-filled eyes. Cardinal Bea could not help proclaiming the event "a miracle! a true miracle!"[6]

JOHN'S SPIRITUAL PREPARATIONS FOR THE COUNCIL

John was not waxing poetic about offering up suffering. On September 23, 1962, doctors had told him he was terminally ill with stomach cancer. Capovilla watched as John calmly discussed the X rays and his gastric pains with the medical men. Already that past summer the pope had told Belgian Cardinal Suenens that he knew his contribution to the council would be suffering. It has been theorized he might have been thinking of the suffering of conflicts and oppositions, rather than of physical suffering. Either way he said and meant, "I am ready for anything."[7]

Besides his own terminal diagnosis, just six days later, on September 29, Giacomo Testa died suddenly at age fifty-three in surgery gone awry. John's public statement, while acknowledging his "true grief," evoked "joyous memories" of one who "served the Church with boundless generosity and made himself loved."[8]

Regarding John's cancer, no public announcement was made. He went on with his ordinary schedule. He had taken initiatives to get every diocese and its parishes, the world's priests and nuns and other groups to pray for the council. His personal spiritual preparations—just before his diagnosis—included a week's prayer retreat. It was, in theory, a retreat in isolation, but there were interruptions. He could only cry, "Lord, you know that I love you," while begging his human deficiencies be shored up by more grace.[9]

On October 4 he again broke with Pius IX's rule that popes stay in the Vatican, going by train on a pilgrimage of prayer for the Council to Loretto and Assisi. It was the first time a pope had done something like that since 1870. From Assisi he spoke to the world about peace and humanity's sharing the world's God-given goods equably. He also gently urged Franciscan childlike simplicity that opens one to the mysteries of God, before which, he said, "human wisdom,…wealth,…domination,…fortune, greatness, politics, power, and prestige…are…shattered."[10]

Bringing the Council to the World—on Radio

The day the council opened, October 11, 1962, John made a radio address to the world. He concentrated on the external aspects of renewal, not the internal Church renewal that was equally important to him. He explained that the council was to renew the Church's encounter with the risen Christ—not just for herself but in order to radiate Christ's light to the world.

Some council themes John mentioned:

- world peace and the basic equality of all peoples
- the world as a family of nations
- marriage and religious-moral aspects of marital procreation, with a call to spouses for generosity and mutual understanding

- the Church as the church of *everyone*—especially the poor[11]

That same day, in St. Peter's, a colorful sea of about twenty five hundred bishops, many with accompanying experts, and patriarchs from various rites flowed into the ancient structure—long lines of men, most in black, reds or purples, wending their slow solemn way down ancient aisles. With the invited ecumenical observers, the 2,905 erected seats were filled.

John came last. To open the council he knelt before the altar, calling on the Holy Spirit in the traditional prayer *Veni Creator*. The following nearly three hours were taken up by a Mass in Latin and Greek, in a gesture of love toward the Eastern rites and Orthodox; the enthroning of Scripture, to make clear Christ's presence and headship over the Church and the council; and other liturgical rites, including the bishops' rite of obedience to the pope.

Finally John stood to speak to the assembly, above all the bishops who were almost all "disposed," as priest Goffredo Zanchi wrote, "to agree with the decisions he would present to them."[12] Few understood that John wanted them to participate actively under the Spirit's direction, not his.

THE SPEECH

John's opening speech, written by himself and titled "Mother Church Rejoices" (*Gaudet Mater Ecclesia*), English biographer Peter Hebblethwaite called it "the speech of his life,"[13] while Italian biographer Zanchi termed it "the fulfillment of wisdom matured through a rich accumulation of lifelong experiences... reread in the light of the Gospel."[14]

No doubt to the surprise of most bishops, John did not tell them what to do. His main points:

- Ecumenical [universal] councils are encounters between Christ and his Church to strengthen the Church's energies and give her right direction. Released will be extraordinary riches of grace and divine assistance. The pope went so far as to call for a new Pentecost.

- While guarding the deposit of faith in its entirety, the Church must look at the present, its changed conditions and ways of living, and leap forward in doctrinal penetration, education of consciences and presentation of perennial truths in ways that people can understand and assimilate.

- Be filled with hope and optimism. Overcome paralyzing pessimism by "turning to the wisdom of history, and the considerations suggested by faith. History... instructs us not to idealize the past to the detriment of the present."

- Trust God. "Providence leads... [to] the fulfillment of God's designs.... The Lord's plans, however hidden they may seem, are for the good of the Church."

- Even human opposition works toward the greater good of the Church.

- Striving toward a unity of souls leading all to peace in this life and salvation in the next, the Church is to be a force for peace, understanding and reconciliation, "a loving mother to all—kind, patient, full of mercy and goodness, even toward the children who are separated from her. To the human race, oppressed by so many difficulties, she says, as did St. Peter to the poor man who asked for alms: 'I have neither silver nor gold, but what I have I give: in the name of Jesus Christ...arise and walk.'"[15]

That fall evening perhaps two hundred thousand people gathered under the pope's window, many of them young. Carrying torches, they formed a huge flaming cross in the darkness.

Monsignor Capovilla recalled suggesting that John speak to them. As a father talking to his children, the pope shared the guiding principal he had learned so long ago from saintly Father Pitocchi: Give all merit to God, and don't think much about yourself.

In total sincerity he continued, "My person counts for nothing. It is your brother who speaks to you, a brother who has become your father by the will of our Lord. But all of this—fatherhood and brotherhood—is a grace from God. All! All!

"Let us...continue to love one another..., going forward making use of what unites us, leaving aside...[what could foster disunity]. We are brothers!"

He told them he did not know how long the council would take but was certain it would bring "outstanding graces." Then he did something unforgettable to most. He asked them, when they went home, to embrace their children and tell them, "This hug is from the pope."[16]

Lest the bishops keep turning to see if the pope were for or against some discussed item, John made the remarkable decision not to be present at the sessions but to watch the proceedings on closed-circuit television. He made a few interventions, such as permitting that discussion be ended ahead of time and a vote taken when enough had been said on a topic. And he saw that bishops from "unimportant" areas were included on the various commissions, whose member selection he sometimes guided minimally to balance representatives who wanted more change with those who wanted little or none. In everything his message continued to be, let the Holy Spirit, not the pope, guide them.

❧ 15 ❧

Of World Rulers and God's Humble Servant

THE COLD WAR, BETWEEN THE COMMUNIST BLOC OF
countries controlled by Russia and the capitalist West led by
the United States, was hot in 1961. The Church under
Communism was martyred, shut down. "The Church of
Silence" was how many referred to it. Like Pius before him,
John suffered and prayed for some way to gain relief for these
Christians, who included "my Bulgarians." But there seemed
no piercing the Iron Curtain, as it was termed, that had
clanged down between the West and Russia following their
joint defeat of the Nazis.

Still, in September Soviet-bloc leader Khrushchev had
spoken well of the pope after a papal radio address. Though
John referred to Khrushchev in his diary on September 20,
1961, as "the despot of Russia" and expressed grave doubts as

to whether the atheist and materialist's sincerity could be believed, these remarks were only in his diary. In *Mater et Magistra* John had verbally cudgeled no one, treating respectfully even those martyring the Church, since they too were created in the image of God. Or as he wrote reflectively in his *Journal*: "My life [as pope] must be filled with the love of Jesus and also with a great outpouring of goodness and sacrifice for individual souls and for the whole world."[1]

AMBASSADOR OF PEACE

In November a telegram of good wishes came from Nikita Khrushchev himself for John's eightieth birthday. John knew this might be a political ploy. But perhaps it gave the pope a finger in the door? Could he pry it open enough that those bishops still alive behind the Iron Curtain could attend the council? Hopeful, he replied to Khrushchev, and a slight relationship of at least surface goodwill was established that would have enormous consequences for the world.

When the East and West powers each resumed nuclear testing, after a tempestuous meeting between Russian and American leaders and subsequent conflict that led to the infamous Berlin Wall, John—carefully not taking sides—spoke out, again inviting world leaders to look to their consciences and the judgment of God and turn toward peace. Khrushchev had his positive response to John's call published in the main Soviet newspapers.

Again John could hope rapport—genuine or feigned[2] as it might be—would ease the sufferings of humanity and the Church of Silence. But there was a price: Some in the West concluded that the pope, who had written in his diary in 1947,

"Between Karl Marx and Jesus Christ an agreement is impossible,"[3] was a Communist sympathizer because he could distinguish between the pernicious doctrine and its followers, despots or no.

As the council opened in October 1962, a year after the pope and the Russian premier had established this slight relationship, Khrushchev and President John F. Kennedy found themselves in a face-off over Communist Cuba's independence and its new nuclear missile sites. The world quivered in fear of nuclear annihilation.

This was only eight months before John's death, "those months. . . a torture," with John in severe pain and Capovilla suffering to see him "reduced to skin and bones." Yet John did not retreat inward. Speaking for all humanity, the pope lifted his voice publicly and in a private message to Khrushchev to urge peace. The papal intervention tipped the scales. Khrushchev credited the Catholic pope with making it possible for him to outface Russia's hawks and retreat from nuclear disaster as "a lover of peace."[4] Capovilla said Kennedy also expressed his gratitude to the pope.

EMERGING FROM THE CHURCH OF SILENCE
As an aftermath to his work for world peace, Pope John also saved one of the Church's own. With Kennedy's approval, American literary man and peace advocate Norman Cousins—who had important contacts in Russia and had played a key role in resolving the Cuban crisis—helped John negotiate with Khrushchev regarding the imprisoned Archbishop Josef Slipyi. Slipyi was head of the crushed Church of Eastern Ukraine, an Eastern rite church in union

with Rome, and one of the Church's *in pectore*, or secret, cardinals. No one knew in what Soviet prison or camp Slipyi was held.

In a face-to-face meeting Cousins assured the Soviet premier on Pope John's behalf that if Khrushchev freed Slipyi, the release "would not be used by the Vatican as anti-Soviet propaganda." In thanks John sent the Church's Protestant negotiator a Russian-style icon of Mary. Cousins "wrote back that his wife and he had received the painting with reverence, kissed it and put it in their bedroom."

Khrushchev sent warm Christmas greetings, and John replied in kind. The main Communist newspaper, *Pravda*, published that note of goodwill toward the Russian people, with its hope for world peace and understanding.

And Khrushchev let it be known he was willing now to allow Christian churches a certain measure of religious freedom. That suffering and persecution might be reduced filled John's heart with unspeakable joy. The night of December 26, he slipped out of bed and, praying ardently before his crucifix, added the conversion of Russia to the other pulls on his heart for which he was offering God his fading life.

A month later word came that Slipyi was being released. True to John's promise not to let this event trigger anti-Soviet sentiment, Capovilla met the Ukrainian quietly at an out-of-the-way train station. He proffered a gift from Pope John: a crucifix.

Slipyi said in good Italian, "If Pope John in his goodness hadn't made this happen, I wouldn't have lived much longer. Cancer was getting the better of me."

The following day the seventy-year-old Slipyi and the

eighty-one-year-old pope recited the *Magnificat* (Luke 1:46–55) together in John's private chapel. Straight from Siberia, Archbishop Slipyi answered John's eager questions about camp conditions and other imprisoned bishops and priests for an hour and a half. Slipyi pointed out camp locations on a map he presented to the pope. For John this was a treasure kept close by until his death. On it he wrote, "The heart is closer to the ones further away; prayer hurries to seek out those in greatest need of understanding and love."

KHRUSHCHEV'S FAMILY COMES CALLING

When Khrushchev's daughter Rada and son-in-law Alexis requested an audience in March 1963, John agreed but was prudent. He told the Vatican newspaper, *L'Osservatore Romano*, to publicize this as a simple, informal exchange of courtesies during which the threesome were never alone: with them was a Jesuit linguist priest who—in addition to writing a full report of all said—interpreted between Alexis and the pope while John spoke to Rada in French. (The pope would also immediately describe the meeting in complete detail to Capovilla so he, too, could write a detailed account, this report the usual source for what was said.) John kept the visit light, reminiscing on his days among the Slavs in Bulgaria and encouraging talk about their three sons, one named Ivan, which is "John" in Russian. "When you return home," the pope said, "give Ivan a hug first. The other two will not mind!"

When his male guest grew serious, suggesting establishing diplomatic relations between the Vatican and Russia, Pope John warmly assured him that this visit was a step on that path but that such relations would take time. For one thing, public opinion needed reshaping. He didn't add that he couldn't recognize one superpower and not the other. An American law of 1867 would block United States and Vatican diplomatic relations until repealed under President Ronald Reagan.

The pope gave Rada a rosary, telling her he prayed these meditation beads each day for the whole world, one decade always being for the children born during that twenty-four-hour period. "Remember [when you look at this]," he said, "that once there was a perfect mother."

The atheist-reared couple left visibly moved. Rada later told an interviewer, "It was perhaps the strongest experience of emotion I have ever felt."[5]

Universally loved, John still had enemies. Someone countermanded his order to the Vatican newspaper, and *no* information about the meeting was released. When the paper was silent, the world press buzzed with precisely the speculation John had prudently tried to avoid: conjectures of his possible intrigue with Communism.

Rather than tracking down and punishing his adversary, John left for history a detailed account of what had occurred. He wrote, "I deplore and pity those who have...lent themselves to unspeakable manoeuvres." Then he added in Latin "I forgive and I put it from my mind."[6]

Whenever John was done a deliberate injury, the same kind of note can be found. He had learned, and practiced as a master, the hardest tenet of Christianity: to forgive those who deliberately act toward you out of malice and—often even harder—to let it go even when severe, long-lasting damage may affect others, in this case potentially his work for world peace.

At this level of holiness, John's spiritual life was simple and serene. The dams of ego fallen long ago, the waters of the Holy Spirit, eternally sparkling and revivifying, kept his soul fresh and young, while weekly confession removed any grit that might clog the flow. His only question now was whether he was hearing the Spirit and obeying aright. The answer seemed to be that he was.

The world was stirred to admiration and many to love. This pope had become what he had asked Rome's diocesan seminarians to pray for, a true "Holy" Father.

JOHN AND THE SAINTS

Clerics who needed John's forgiveness were not all in the Vatican. In southern Italy there were those, including a bishop, who wanted to destroy mystic stigmatist Franciscan (today Saint) Padre Pio. They thought to do this through John. They sent the pope "evidence," compromising photos showing Pio—whose purity was actually of the same angelic level as John's—with women.[7]

John's old friend Andrea Cesarano, for thirty years the archbishop of Manfredonia, came to visit him in 1961 and found the habitually genial John strangely perturbed.

"What can you tell me about Padre Pio?" the pope asked abruptly.

"Holiness," Cesarano began, only to be interrupted.

"Don't call me 'Holiness.' Call me Angelo, the way you always have. Tell me about him!"

"Don Angelo, Padre Pio is forever the man of God I've known since I was transferred... [south]. He's an apostle who does immense good to souls."

"Don Andrea, here I hear bad things about Padre Pio," John exclaimed.

"Calumnies! I've known Padre Pio since 1933, and I assure you he is always God's man, a saint!"

The pope brought out a photo. Familiar with this sort of thing, Cesarano showed John how it was clearly a fake, made by photographing together two separate pictures.

Further discussion, including Cesarano's telling John about an encounter of his own sister with Padre Pio, ended in the archbishop's quick dispatch to repeat what he knew of Pio to Cardinals Ottaviano and Tardini before the next day's convening of the Holy Office to discuss Pio's "case." God had kept one saint from causing enormous harm to another.[8]

That was fitting for—although none of his favorites were associated with sensational phenomena like Pio's—John was a man who loved "the cloud of witnesses" (Hebrews 12:1), the saints. While it was always Jesus Christ who was the center of his life, Angelo Giuseppe Roncalli had been reared to call upon the prayer intercession of Saint Joseph and Saint John the Baptist, for whom so many Roncallis were named. He was also raised with devotion to the motherly prayer intercession of Jesus' mother, Mary. Besides putting out an encyclical on the devotion most connected to Mary, the rosary, he wrote his own rosary meditations on Jesus' and his mother's lives. (Capovilla published these after John's death).

From youth he had taken as examples great followers of Christ such as Francis of Assisi and Bishops Saint Charles Borromeo and Saint Francis de Sales. All that religious art in the papal bedroom included representations (think of them as photos) of these and other saints, along with beautiful icons and paintings of Mother Mary.

One of the first things he had done on becoming pope was to add Saint Joseph to the saints who are honored and whose prayers are invoked in every Mass. During his brief pontificate he beatified a number of European men and women, as well as American wife, mother and Sister of Charity, Elizabeth Ann Seton, the first American citizen to be so honored. As a priest himself of Bergamo, he found great satisfaction in canonizing seventeenth-century Bergamo bishop Gregory Barbarigo. And on February 10, 1963, he signed the decree that set in motion official recognition of the holiness of his spiritual father, Cardinal Andrea Ferrari. John XXIII's Milan mentor would be beatified by Pope John Paul II in 1987.

In 1911 Roncalli had written an article on saintly Bergamo priest Don Luigi Maria Palazzolo, founder of the Sisters of the Poor. In 1927 he was among the bishops petitioning Rome for Palazzolo's enlistment in the rolls of official saints. Following verification by medical commissions that healings attributed to Palazzolo's prayers were miraculous, John's long efforts to help the Sisters of the Poor were crowned with success. With only two months and fifteen days to live, he beatified Luigi Maria Palazzolo and brought a final honor to his native diocese.

❧ 16 ❧

Go in Peace

CAPOVILLA RECALLS THAT ON OCTOBER 25, 1962, WHILE appealing for negotiations during the Cuban missile crisis, the dying pope recognized the urgent need to summon humanity—while he still could—to a better peace. In that moment in the Cold War, peace—defined as the absence of nuclear conflict—rested on the justly dubbed "balance of terror," each side holding back for fear the other could unleash *their* nuclear arsenal before annihilation.

John set to work on the last of his six encyclicals, *Pacem in Terris* ("Peace on Earth"), telling the monsignor helping him, "I can't attribute ill will to anyone or there'll be no dialogue at all." So the encyclical just says, "There exists in man's very nature an undying capacity to break through barriers of error and seek the road to truth,"[1] without specifying that Communism was in error.

Pacem in Terris appeared on April 19, 1963, when John had six weeks to live. Breaking with tradition, it was addressed not to Catholics but to "all...of Good Will." Acknowledging that there can be no peace without justice, John exhorted the world to dialogue on issues of justice, including the right to freedom of worship.

He asked humanity to recognize moves toward greater human dignity: the working class achieving more rights; women gaining consideration as persons, including some as paid workers; colonialism on a trajectory toward nations' independence and racism toward human equality.

John asked Catholics to distinguish between philosophical doctrines and socioeconomic movements. The first are fixed; the second, like people, can be influenced and changed, even radically. He also urged Catholics to remain true to Christian doctrine and the Church's social teachings but not to fear prudent collaboration with movements in order to foster humanity's well-being and peace.

While there were some cries that John was a Communist or Communist dupe, the encyclical received enormous acclaim from the world's anxious peoples, East and West. Khrushchev lauded it, while, Capovilla says, American president John F. Kennedy found the courage to say, "This encyclical makes me proud to be Catholic." Maybe the *Washington Post* got it right: They called Pope John the "voice of the world's conscience."[2]

And the voice was heard: Two months after John died, offering his death for peace among other goods, Khrushchev and Kennedy signed a nuclear test ban.

Meantime for his work toward peace in the world, the pope received the Balzan Prize for Humanity, Peace and

Brotherhood Among Peoples from a European foundation. The Curia were mostly against John's accepting it, and with good reason: The pope had only been doing the duty of Christ's vicar, and popes should be above prizes, particularly, said those concerned with papal dignity, ones little known beyond Europe.

Pale and in terrible pain—which he managed to hide fairly well—John accepted the prize because his friend, Giovanni Battista Montini, urged he do so. And he saw Montini, by whatever light, as his soon-to-be successor. The large sum that came with the award the pope donated to a Vatican fund for peace activities.

STILL ASCENDING

As Lent of 1963 arrived, Pope John continued visiting Rome's parishes in the outlying, least pious districts. On one of these trips, Capovilla worried aloud that John might hemorrhage. The secretary never forgot the serene reply: "So I die in the street. Don't many other Christians do the same?"

On Good Friday, exhausted by pain, John was nevertheless at St. Peter's for veneration of the cross. The day after Easter his diary noted "continual pain" and the honest appraisal: "actually in very bad shape." Yet he recorded "contentment" and "abandonment in God," and he read over the texts for the bishops' second session.

At his last public audience, on May 15, noticeably thinner and the terrible pain undiminished, his pale face was lit by interior joy. Suddenly, he exclaimed almost gaily that those present were not in St. Peter's for a funeral but that even funerals were a joy.

"Oh, the Hail Mary," he continued with animation, "the Hail Mary! The first Hail Mary of the toddler, the final Hail Mary of the dying!"

Two days later he said his last Mass. After that Capovilla said Mass each day in the study next to the pope's bedroom, giving John Communion in bed as he lay facing the crucifix on the opposite wall. Yet the following Sunday, May 19, the dying man got up and went to the balcony to pray the *Regina Coeli* with the flock, his voice strong, filled with a love he could only express by the unheard-of papal gesture of blowing the crowd kisses.

On Wednesday, May 22, hemorrhages began, leading to transfusions, intravenous feeding and other interventions. Yet he managed a last audience with some bishops. Again he was at the window that day, talking one last time to the faithful. Fittingly it was the vigil of Jesus' ascension, and he said, "Let us run behind the Divine Master as he ascends."[3]

He tried to recite the *Regina Coeli* with the crowd, but their applause—perhaps sensing this was the last time they would see him—made this impossible. Capovilla saw the Holy Father was deeply moved.

On May 23, the now white-haired Gustavo Testa, friend of fifty years, was bedside. Sobbing, he was comforted by John. The pope also thought tenderly of his beloved family and thanked Capovilla for considerations the secretary had given the Roncallis.

Telegrams poured into the Vatican expressing love, prayers, respect and appreciation. *L'Osservatore Romano* obeyed the pope's request to reply to his well-wishers that he was ready to offer his life for the Church, the council and humanity's aspirations for peace. If their prayers obtained more time for him, he hoped they would help him and his coworkers become holy in order to work for the coming of God's kingdom.

When not absorbed in prayer, he asked to hear pages from his beloved *Imitation of Christ* or from *Fire of Love*, the book he'd been reading by a seventeenth-century Capuchin mystic.

He was still ascending.

The world's prayer pleas for this aged "father of everyone" came from non-Christians too. Among those gathered in St. Peter's Square, for instance, were a group of observant Jews led by the chief rabbi of Rome, Elio Toaff. Slightly over a year earlier, on March 17, 1962, John's car had been passing the Roman synagogue just as services ended. As Rabbi Toaff stood in the doorway and his congregation poured out, John told his driver to stop. Wanting to express respect and friendship, smiling broadly, John blessed the Jews. Wanting equally to show respect and affection for the pope's gesture of goodwill, the Jewish congregants surrounded the papal car and applauded.

And that is why, as John lay dying, a group of Roman Jews joined people of every persuasion keeping vigil for him.

APOGEE

Near midnight on May 30, the cancer perforated the stomach, causing intense pain. A shaken Capovilla, trying not to weep, told John he was dying. His serene reply: "Help me to die as a bishop, as a pope should."[4]

The next three days, in and out of consciousness, he remained at peace and in prayer. He said good-bye to cardinals who happened to be in Rome, including Montini.

Some of his beloved family arrived.

Gazing at "the secret of my life," the crucifix hanging across from his bed, John said, "He died for everyone; no one is rejected from his love, from his forgiveness."[5] Aware, he said, more than ever in his inner dialogue with Christ of the urgency of the world's redemption, he prayed repeatedly Jesus' prayer, *Ut unum sint* ("That they may be one"). After receiving last rites, he affirmed again that he offered his life for Christian unity, the Church, the council, world peace...

At one of their morning visits, he reminded his closest coworkers, secretary of state Cardinal Cicognani and undersecretary Angelo Dell'Acqua, of an insight he had shared with them at the opening of the council: "It is not the Gospel that has changed; it is we who begin to understand it better."[6]

Understanding it far, far more than could be told in words, John XXIII, born Angelo Giuseppe Roncalli, passed out of this world—his relatives, Capovilla and the little household family all there by the bed—at 7:45 PM on the summer's evening of June 3, 1963. Over the loudspeaker in St. Peter's Square came the Latin words *Ite Missa Est*.[7] They signified the end of the Mass being said for John in the presence of an immense crowd of believers and nonbelievers, members of the human family gathered there because they loved him.

Epilogue

THOSE ATTENDING THE SECOND VATICAN COUNCIL called for reviving ancient custom and enlisting John in the rolls of the saints by acclamation. But proponents of the formal, quasi-juridical process, in use now for centuries, prevailed.

So the Process, as it is called, began. Those who knew him over his lifetime in the various places he lived gave testimony under oath. Those testifying included Fritz von Papen, there because Roncalli's letter had saved his life during the Nuremberg Trials.

With large numbers alive to testify from knowledge up close and personal, the investigation left no doubt that John XXIII had practiced the Christian virtues heroically. The formal account of his life that was prepared agreed. And his huge number of writings, sifted to see if he led others away from truth or showed lack of virtue, concurred. As Capovilla would put it in 2008, here was a man who—from his humility and meekness, chastity, devotion and affability—imaged goodness.[1]

Heroic virtue—formally proclaimed and giving the individual the title of venerable, that is, one worthy of veneration—makes a person worthy, as an imitator of Christ, of being held up for others to imitate (see 1 Corinthians 4:16; Philippians 3:17; 1 Thessalonians 1:6). One may also safely ask his prayers.

Someone did. I summarize the story of this member of the Daughters of Charity.

Although she was still a young woman, Sister Caterina Capitani's internal bleeding from ulcers went back years. As a radical remedy, three-quarters of her stomach and her spleen were removed in 1965. In May 1966 the quarter stomach she had left developed a peptic ulcer complicated by a fistula, that is, an open running sore, which broke through her abdomen, emitting everything she ate.

Her pulse weak, her breathing labored, her temperature high and the fistula making normal nourishment impossible, Sister Caterina was close to death. She received the last rites and, at her request, was left alone in her hospital room to pray.

Saying her rosary, she suddenly felt a hand on her ravaged stomach, while a man's voice said her name. The sudden touch and voice frightened her. Nervously she rolled over and saw Pope John "smiling and incredibly beautiful" at her side.

"Don't be afraid," he told her. "It's all over. You're well." They spoke together for about ten minutes. Although much of what was said remains Caterina's secret, it is known that the dead pope told the nun the fistula would close up and she'd be able to eat anything she wanted.

When he left, the joy-filled sister found her pain, fever and all other symptoms gone too. As for the fistula, a tiny black dot pinpointed where it had been, as if to aid medical men in judging this miracle. (Fistulas *can* close but not instantaneously.)

Sister Caterina leapt out of bed, excitedly calling for something to eat. Within forty-eight hours, nourishment restored her strength to the point that she went back to her demanding work as a nurse. From that time on she had none of the digestive problems that ought to have remained in her case.[2]

After an investigation for the cause for canonization finds heroic sanctity, the Church waits for miracles as a sign of God's desire that this particular person be held up as a role model through beatification.[3] The required sign from God of *his* desire that Venerable John XXIII's holiness be officially recognized was given with Sister Caterina's cure in 1966, only three years after the pope's holy death. Some would say that the Master of the universe even underlined the point by sending the dead pope as the messenger of God's healing.

This after-death appearance was not the only unusual thing that was part of the process toward John's September 3, 2000, beatification. When his unembalmed remains were exhumed for official identification, the body was found incorrupt.[4]

Notes

All material without a source note comes from Archbishop Capovilla's communications, primarily by personal interviews with the author.

CHAPTER 1: BEGINNINGS

1. This description and other material may be found in José Luis González-Balado with Loris F. Capovilla, *Il Cuore di Papa Giovanni. Aneddoti di una vita* (Milan: PIMEdit ONLUS, 2002) (hereafter *Il Cuore*), p. 200.
2. As quoted in *Il Cuore*, p. 200.
3. Giovanni XXIII, *Lettere ai familiari, 1901–1962*, ed. Loris Capovilla (Rome: Storia e Letteratura, 1968) (hereafter *Lettere*), p. 8n.
4. *Lettere*, vol. 1, p. 283.
5. See Pope John XXIII, *Journal of a Soul* (New York: McGraw-Hill, 1965) (hereafter *Journal*), p. 412.
6. Quoted in Mario Benigni and Goffredo Zanchi, *John XXIII: The Official Biography* (Boston: Pauline, 2001), p. 145.
7. Benigni and Zanchi, p. 28.
8. Pope John XXIII, *Il Giornale dell'Anima*, ed. Alberto Melloni (Bologna: Istituto per le scienze religiose, 1987) (hereafter *Giornale*), p. 136.
9. *Lettere*, vol. 1, p. 298.
10. *Lettere*, vol. 1, p. 144
11. *Journal*, p. 89.
12. *Journal*, p. 82.
13. See *Journal*, retreat notes of 1897, p. 17.
14. *Giornale*, p. 177.
15. *Journal*, p. 94.
16. *Journal*, p. 88
17. Loris Capovilla, "Chronology, 1881–1963," in *Journal*, p. xxxviii.

CHAPTER 2: FORMATION IN ROME

1. *Lettere*, vol. 1, pp. 3–4.
2. *Journal*, p. 415.
3. *Journal*, p. 86.
4. *Journal*, p. 102.
5. *Journal*, p. 86.
6. Letter to his rector in Rome, quoted in Benigni and Zanchi, p. 49.
7. Roncalli personal archives at Sotto il Monte, quoted in Benigni and Zanchi, p. 51.
8. *Journal*, pp. 86–89. Sixty years later he summed it all up as the fight against self-love, as quoted by Capovilla in his introduction to *Journal*, p. xvii.
9. *Journal*, p. 90.

10. *Journal*, p. 84n2.
11. *Journal*, pp. 85–86.
12. *Journal*, p. 21.
13. *Journal*, pp. 78–79.
14. *Journal*, p. 108.
15. Capovilla, Introduction, *Journal*, p. xvii.
16. Quoted in Benigni and Zanchi, p. 31. See personal notes in *Journal* and other pious writings from June 1897.
17. *Journal*, p. 55.
18. Quoted in Angelo Roncalli, "A Tribute to the Memory of Father Francesco Pitocchi," in *Journal*, p. 431.
19. *Journal*, p. 101.
20. *Journal*, pp. 111–112.
21. Roncalli, "Tribute," in *Journal*, p. 437.
22. *Journal*, p. 136.
23. *Journal*, p. 160.
24. *Lettere*, vol. 1, p. 17.
25. *Journal*, pp. 160–161.
26. *Journal*, p. 161.
27. *Journal*, p. 161.
28. *Journal*, p. 162.
29. See Benigni and Zanchi, p. 59.

CHAPTER 3: A PRIEST OF BERGAMO
1. Letter to G. Signor, January 11, 1905, from the episcopal archives of Bergamo, quoted variously, including Benigni and Zanchi, p. 63.
2. Angelo Giuseppe Roncalli, *My Bishop: A Portrait of Mgr Giacomo Maria Radini Tedeschi*, Dorothy White, trans. (London: Geoffrey Chapman, 1969), p. 48, quoted in Peter Hebblethwaite, *Pope John XXIII: Shepherd of the Modern World* (New York: Doubleday, 1985), p. 51.
3. *Journal*, p. 169.
4. Benigni and Zanchi, p. 75.
5. Benigni and Zanchi, pp. 76, 78.
6. *Journal*, p. 169.
7. Diary, March 1, 1917, quoted in Benigni and Zanchi, p. 129.
8. *L'Eco di Bergamo*, December 5, 1907, quoted in Benigni and Zanchi, p. 79.
9. Benigni and Zanchi, p. 80.
10. Benigni and Zanchi, p. 86.
11. *Journal*, p. 411.
12. *Journal*, pp. 171, 173.
13. *Journal*, pp. 173–174.
14. *Journal*, p. 180.
15. Angelo Roncalli, "Ricordando don Luigi Palozzolo," *La Vita Diocesana*, Bergamo, 1911, Appendix in *Ottima e reverenda madre: Lettere di papa Giovanni alle suore*, ed. Giambattista Busetti (Bologna: Dehoniane, 1990), p. 381.

16. *Journal*, p. 184.
17. *Journal*, p. 178.
18. *Journal*, p. 181.
19. *Journal*, p. 180.
20. *Journal*, p. 178.

CHAPTER 4: DRAMA, DEATHS AND A WORLD WAR I CHAPLAINCY

1. *Journal*, pp. 175–176.
2. Letter of June 2, 1914, quoted in Benigni and Zanchi, p. 106.
3. Benigni and Zanchi, p. 106.
4. Some sources relate that Pius said this to German and French efforts; others cite an ambassador from Austria. Whether he said these exact words and, if so, to whom, it is completely accurate from all he said and did to use them to sum up his acts and attitude.
5. *Journal*, pp. 183–184.
6. Angelo Roncalli, *In memoria di Msgr. Giacomo M. Radini Tedeschi, Vescovo di Bergamo* (Rome: Storia e Letteratura, 1963), p. 204, quoted in Benigni and Zanchi, p. 109.
7. Roncalli, *In memoria*, p. 206, quoted in Benigni and Zanchi, p. 110.
8. Roncalli, *In memoria*, p. 219, quoted in Benigni and Zanchi, p. 110.
9. Roncalli, *In memoria*, p. 219, quoted in Benigni and Zanchi, p. 110.
10. See *Lettere*, vol. 1, p. 25.
11. See Benigni and Zanchi, p. 110.
12. *Journal*, p. 184.
13. *Journal*, p. 186.
14. *Journal*, p. 187.
15. The book is titled *In memoria di Msgr. Giacomo M. Radini Tedeschi, Vescovo di Bergamo*.
16. Entry in his diary for March 17, 1917, quoted in Benigni and Zanchi, p. 122.
17. All quotes in this paragraph are from his diary entry of July 10, 1918, the full text of which is quoted in Benigni and Zanchi, p. 123.
18. *Il Rosario con papa Giovanni*, p. 126, gives the text of a postwar speech at Lourdes; one may read the same phrase in another talk in Hebblethwaite, p. 83.
19. *Lettere*, vol. 1, p. 61.
20. Diary, July 29, 1918, quoted in Benigni and Zanchi, p. 124.
21. Letter to D. Spolverini, August 2 or 4, 1918, quoted in Benigni and Zanchi, p. 124.

CHAPTER 5: TEACHER AND GUIDE

1. *Journal*, p. 194.
2. *Journal*, p. 193.
3. Diary entry for Sunday, November 9, 1919, quoted in Benigni and Zanchi, p. 131.
4. Diary entry for April 12, 1920, quoted in Benigni and Zanchi, p. 133.
5. Diary, quoted in Benigni and Zanchi, p. 121.
6. Quoted in Benigni and Zanchi, p. 136.
7. Diary entry for November 16, 1919, quoted in Benigni and Zanchi, p. 137.

8. See "Benedetto XV nei ricordi de Giovanni XXIII," *L'Osservatore Romano*, January 22, 1959, p. 3, quoted in Walter H. Peters, *The Life of Benedict XV* (Milwaukee: Bruce, 1959), p. 252n.

9. Letter from Cardinal Andrea Ferrari, December 17, 1920, quoted in Benigni and Zanchi, p. 140, citing L. Algisi, *Papa Giovanni*, p. 416.

10. Diary, December 19, 1920, quoted in Benigni and Zanchi, p. 140.

CHAPTER 6: AT HOME IN ROME

1. *Lettere*, vol. 1, Rome III, p. 79.

2. Quoted in Benigni and Zanchi, p. 153. Facts on the visit and the religious congregation are in *Ottima e reverenda madre*, p. 163.

3. Diary, February 8, 1924, quoted in Benigni and Zanchi, p. 155.

4. *Journal*, p. 198.

5. *Journal*, p. 198.

6. See letter to Cardinal G. van Rossum, February 23, 1925, quoted in Benigni and Zanchi, p. 159.

7. *Journal*, p. 204.

8. *Journal*, p. 206.

CHAPTER 7: BULGARIAN EXILE

1. May 29, 1925, letter to Gustavo Testa, quoted in Benigni and Zanchi, p. 162.

2. Letter dated January 15, 1931, quoted in Benigni and Zanchi, pp. 179–180.

3. *Ottima e reverenda madre*, pp. 13, 14.

4. A 1933 letter, quoted in Benigni and Zanchi, p. 183.

5. Letter to seminarian Christo Morcefki in 1926, quoted in Benigni and Zanchi, p. 186.

6. *Lettere*, vol. 1, pp. 157–158.

7. *Lettere*, vol. 1, pp. 195–196.

8. Benigni and Zanchi, p. 184, quoting a letter written April 2, 1933.

9. See *Il Cuore*, pp. 249–253.

10. *Lettere*, vol. 1, various letters, pp. 188–189, 220, 229.

11. *Lettere*, vol. 1, p. 218

12. *Lettere*, vol. 1, p. 218

13. *Lettere*, vol. 1, p. 171.

14. Benigni and Zanchi, p. 181.

15. Cardinal Sincero shared Pope Pius XI's words to Sincero with Roncalli. See Giovanni XXIII, *Giornale dell'Anima* (Rome: Storia e Letteratura, 1964), p. 387, quoted in Benigni and Zanchi, p. 188.

16. *Il Cuore*, p. 77.

CHAPTER 8: TURKEY AND GREECE

1. Benigni and Zanchi, p. 188.

2. *Lettere,* vol. 1, p. 333.

3. Robert L. Stern, "A Visit to Turkey and Its Christian Communities, *One*, November 2005, p. 28, available at www.cnewa.org. *One* is the official publication of Catholic Near East Welfare Association.

4. See *Lettere*, vol. 1, pp. 353–361.
5. Giustino Farnedi, ed., *Giovanni XXIII: Lettere Familiari* (Milan: Piemme, 1993), letter 338.
6. Hebblethwaite, p. 245, citing Bruno Bertoli, *La Questione Romana negli Scritti di Papa Giovanni* (Brescia: Morcelliana, 1970), pp. 18–20.
7. *Lettere*, vol. 1, p. 408.
8. *Journal*, p. 246.
9. *Lettere*, vol. 1, p. 447.
10. Congregation for the Causes of Saints, *Beatificationis et canonizationis servi Dei Ionnis Papae XXIII, summi pontificis (1881–1963), Positio super vita, virtuibus et fama sanctitatis*, vol. 4 (Rome: n.p., 1996), p. 1020, quoted in Benigni and Zanchi, p. 194.

CHAPTER 9: WALKING WORLD WAR II'S TIGHTROPE

1. *Lettere*, vol. 1, pp. 544, 571.
2. Hebblethwaite, p. 165, quoting Loris Capovilla, *Giovanni XXIII, Quidici Letture* [fifteen lectures on Pope John XXIII] (Rome: Storia e Letteratura, 1970), p. 286.
3. *Lettere*, vol. 1, p. 568.
4. See Ronald J. Rychlak, *Hitler, the War, and the Pope* (Huntington, Ind.: Our Sunday Visitor, 2000), p. 253. Most Italian Jews were saved because, under Pius XII's quiet orders, convents, monasteries, the Vatican itself and other Church institutions hid them or helped them leave the country. Rabbi David G. Dalin, author of *The Myth of Hitler's Pope: How Pope Pius XII Rescued Jews From the Nazis* (Regnery, 2005), reports, for instance, that Pius, whose great friend as a boy was a Jew—whom he saved—had three thousand Jews hidden in Castel Gandolfo, the papal summer residence, besides all those stuffed inside the Vatican and those openly hired by Pius when Fascist anti-Semitic laws terminated their jobs. Were there Catholic anti-Semites? There certainly were. But Pius XII was not among them
5. Dutch Protestant and Catholic bishops planned to have read from every pulpit a statement against the Nazi invaders' anti-Semitism. The Nazis warned of reprisal, and the Protestants prudently backed down. The pastoral letter was read in every Catholic church. The reprisal was not arrest of the bishops but first immediate arrest and murder of all Catholics of Jewish descent. Nor was that the end: Rabbi Dalin quotes Israeli historian Pinchas Lapide, who had been a diplomat in Italy during the war, that while the Dutch hierarchy spoke out more than any other against the persecution of Jews, the Nazis responded by having more Jews from the Netherlands deported to death camps than from any other country, 79 percent (see Dalin, p. 79, quoting Pinchas Lapide, *Three Popes and the Jews* [New York: Hawthorn, 1967], p. 27). The two Jewish scholars conclude that the open opposition, so well meant, was a mistake.
6. *Actes et Documents du Saint-Siège relatifs à la second guerre mondiale*, p. 306.
7. Benigni and Zanchi, p. 204, citing a note written by Roncalli about their meetings.

8. *Ottima e reverenda madre*, pp. 257–258; a longer quote in English from this letter is in Benigni and Zanchi, p. 202.

9. *Actes et Documents du Saint-Siège*, p. 271, quoted in Benigni and Zanchi, p. 203.

10. See Stephane Groueff, *Crown of Thorns: The Reign of King Boris III of Bulgaria 1918–1943* (Lanham, Md.: Madison, 1987) for a discussion of Boris's mysterious death after being given an untenable order by the losing Hitler to send Bulgarians to fight in Russia and being told, equally untenably, by the Allies that to come over to that side, he had to accept Stalin and Russia. Whether his illness was of the heart from stress or, as his German doctors thought, poison—there is equal reason to suspect the Allies as well as the Axis side—is unknown.

11. Benigni and Zanchi, p. 204, quoting *Actes et Documents du Saint-Siège*, p. 189, emphasis mine.

12. See *Il Cuore*, pp. 139–140.

13. Loris Capovilla, ed., *Giovanni e Paolo, due papi: Saggio di corrispondenza (1925-1962)* (Rome: Studium, 1982), p. 29.

14. Capovilla's introduction to *Giovanni e Paolo*, p. 17.

15. *Journal*, p. 251.

16. *Journal*, p. 237.

17. *Journal*, p. 239.

18. See *Journal*, pp. 238–239.

19. *Journal*, p. 237.

20. *Journal*, p. 245.

21. *Journal*, p. 255.

22. *Journal*, p. 250.

CHAPTER 10: THE PARIS YEARS

1. *Il Cuore*, p. 155.

2. Capovilla, *Giovanni e Paolo*, pp. 37–38.

3. Benigni and Zanchi, p. 222.

4. *Il Cuore*, pp. 33–34.

5. Angelo Giuseppe Roncalli, *Souvenirs d'un Nonce: Cahiers de France (1944–1953)* (Rome: Storia e Letteratura, 1963), p. 143, as quoted in Benigni and Zanchi, p. 226.

6. *Souvenirs d'un Nonce*, p. 143.

7. Benigni and Zanchi, p. 226, quoting Quai d'Orsay archives.

8. See Benigni and Zanchi, p. 225.

9. *Lettere*, vol. 2, Paris, p. 78.

10. The diary entries are quoted in Benigni and Zanchi, p. 230.

11. *Souvenirs d'un Nonce*, p. 169.

12. *Lettere*, vol. 2, p. 117.

13. *Lettere*, vol. 2, p. 14.

14. *Lettere*, vol. 2, p. 9.

15. *Souvenirs d'un Nonce*, p. 138.

16. Hebblethwaite, p. 225.

17 *Lettere*, vol. 2, p. 210.

18. *Lettere*, vol. 2, p. 116.

19. See *Lettere*, vol. 2, p. 10.

20. *Souvenirs d'un Nonce*, pp. 69–70.

21. *Souvenirs d'un Nonce*, p. 74.

22. See *Souvenirs d'un Nonce*, p. xiv.

23. From interview and *Il Cuore*, vol. 6, pp. 88–89.

24. *Journal*, pp. 107–108.

25. See *Souvenirs d'un Nonce*, pp. 160, 164, 170, 179 for samples of books given him and pp. 36–37 for samples of his quotes from LaFontaine.

26. *Lettere*, vol. 2, p. 235.

27. Farnedi, p. 316.

28. *Lettere*, vol. 2, p. 39.

29. Farnedi, p. 338, quoting letter from Istanbul, December 2, 1935.

30. Henri Fesquet, *Wit and Wisdom of Good Pope John*, trans. Salvator Attanasio (New York: Signet, 1965), p. 40.

31. Circulating orally in various versions, one slightly different account of this may be found in Fesquet, p. 67.

32. Loris Capovilla, ed., *Pasqua di risurrezione con papa Giovanni XXIII* (Rome: Storia e Letteratura, 1978), p. 29, as quoted in Hebblethwaite, p. 233.

33. *Lettere*, vol. 2, pp. 302–303, 307.

CHAPTER 11: SHEPHERD OF VENICE

1. Capovilla, *Giovanni XXIII*, p. 37; *Journal*, p. 282.

2. *Journal*, p. 282.

3. *Il Cuore*, p. 121.

4. *Journal*, p. 285n.

5   *Lettere*, vol. 2, p. 370.

6. *Journal*, p. 283.

7. *Lettere*, vol. 2, p. 372.

8. *Journal*, p. 352, emphasis added.

9. Capovilla, *Giovanni XXIII*, p. 50.

10. *Lettere*, vol. 2, p. 364.

11. Letter of August 12, 1956, from *Scritti e discorsi 1953–1958* (Rome: Paoline, 1959–1962), pp. 456–457, quoted in Benigni and Zanchi, p. 266.

12. *Scritti e discorsi*, quoted in Benigni and Zanchi, p 267.

13. Benigni and Zanchi, p. 269.

14. Benigni and Zanchi, p. 268; see also p. 269 for message and analysis.

15. Benigni and Zanchi, p. 269.

16. *Lettere*, vol. 2, p. 387.

17 *Lettere*, vol. 2, p. 425.

18. *Journal*, p. 283.

19. *Lettere*, vol. 2, p. 409.

20. *Lettere*, vol. 2, p. 368.

CHAPTER 12: RETURN TO ROME

1. See *Journal*, p. 325.
2. *Il Cuore*, p. 39.
3. Loris Capovilla, *Vent' anni dalla elezione di Giovanni XXIII*, p. 45.
4. *Journal*, p. 299.
5. *Journal*, p. 310.
6. *Discorsi, messagi, colloqui del Santo Padre Giovanni XXIII*, 5 volumes, (Vatican: Polyglot, 1958–1963), vol. I, pp. 3–4.
7. *Il Cuore*, p. 136.
8. *Discorsi, messagi, colloqui*, vol. I, pp. 10–14, quoted in Benigni and Zanchi, p. 284.
9. *Il Cuore*, pp. 235–236.
10. Capovilla, *Giovanni e Paolo*, p. 100.
11. Capovilla, *Giovanni e Paolo*, p. 104 .
12. Description in a letter dated January 30, 2007, to the author from Thomas F. Stransky, C.S.P., of the Tantur Ecumenical Institute, Jerusalem, who worked with Testa during John's papacy in Rome. In a 1930s photo Testa was slim.
13. As quoted in Capovilla, *Vent'anni dalla elezione*, p. 45.
14. *Il Cuore*, pp. 48–49, contains Capovilla's description of the seminary visit.
15. See Benigni and Zanchi, pp. 313–314.
16. 2007 letter from a superior of the order, quoting Sister Primarosa.
17. Capovilla, *Vent'anni dalla elezione*, p. 46, quoted in Benigni and Zanchi, p. 289.
18. *Lettere*, vol. 2, pp. 447–450.
19. Fesquet, pp. 32–33.
20. *Il Rosario con papa Giovanni*, p. 6, quoting *L'Osservatore Romano*, December 9–10, 1961.

CHAPTER 13: A FATHERLY HOLY FATHER

1. Essay by Madeleine Delbrêl, "Noi, delle strade" (Gribaudi, 1969), quoted in Loris Capovilla, foreword to Benigni and Zanchi, pp. xv–xvi.
2. Fesquet, p. 17.
3. *Il Cuore*, p. 45.
4. Leon-Joseph Cardinal Suenens, *Memories and Hopes* (Dublin: Veritas, 1992), quoted in *Il Cuore*, p. 214.
5. *Il Cuore*, p. 148 has this reminiscence.
6. See Capovilla's much longer account of the pope and Grente's relationship in *Il Cuore*, pp. 164–165.
7. Interview printed in *Il Cuore*, vol. 8, p. 163.
8. *Il Cuore*, p. 164.
9. *Il Cuore*, p. 171.
10. *Il Cuore*, p. 132.
11. An anecdote from longtime Vatican correspondent Arcangelo Paglialunga, reported in *Il Cuore*, pp. 132–133.
12. *Il Cuore*, p. 134.
13. Foreword, Benigni and Zanchi, p. xv.
14. *Il Cuore*, p. 133.

15. Pope John XXIII, *Mater et Magistra*, May 15, 1961, no. 238, www.osjspm.org.
16. In the twenty-first century, regarding the authenticity or "myths" of the Scriptures, factions are still at war within both Catholicism and Protestantism. Few demythologizers study modern saints, in whose lives are well-verified duplications of many of Christ's miracles.
17. 1962 letter to Cardinal Tisserant, quoted in Benigni and Zanchi, p. 329.
18. See *Journal*, p. 308.

CHAPTER 14: THE COUNCIL

1. Marco Roncalli did two interviews with Zenit, the second, this one, on November 26, 2006, available at www.ewtn.com.
2. Fellow Augustinian Father Robert Gavotto, as a seminarian in Rome during John's papacy, heard Van Lierde say this. Van Lierde was a papal official and lived in the Vatican.
3. From the Agenda Notes for Vatican Council II, p. 47, quoted in Benigni and Zanchi, p. 357.
4. Giulio Bevilacqua, "Meditation," in *Journal*, p. xxvii.
5. Stjepan Schmidt, *Augustin Bea: The Cardinal of Unity*, trans. Leslie Wearne (New Rochelle, N.Y.: New City, 1992), p. 744.
6. Quoted in Schmidt, p. 454. At his press conference on November 9, 1962, Cardinal Bea enlarged on his comment, saying the miracle also included the two years of experiences that had led up to the meeting.
7. *Journal*, p. 319.
8. Farnedi, pp. 364–365.
9. *Journal*, p. 325.
10. *Discorsi, messagi, colloqui*, vol. 4, p. 557, quoted in Benigni and Zanchi, p. 386.
11. *Discorsi, messagi, colloqui*, vol. 4, pp. 521, 523, listed in Benigni and Zanchi, p. 389.
12. Benigni and Zanchi, p. 389.
13. Hebblethwaite, p. 535.
14. Benigni and Zanchi, pp. 390–391.
15. Pope John XXIII, *Gaudet Mater Ecclesia*, as quoted in Benigni and Zanchi, pp. 392–394.
16. Capovilla's memories and *Discorsi, messagi, colloqui*, vol. 4, pp. 592–593.

CHAPTER 15: OF WORLD RULERS AND GOD'S HUMBLE SERVANT

1. *Journal*, p. 317.
2. Marco Roncalli's first interview with Zenit, November 24, 2006, www.ewtn.com.
3. Diary, October 28, 1947, quoted in Benigni and Zanchi, p. 234.
4. Hebblethwaite, quoting what Khrushchev told Kennedy's confidant Norman Cousins, p. 447.
5. A very detailed account by Capovilla may be found in *Il Cuore*, pp. 218–220.
6. Giancarlo Zizola, *L'Utopia di Papa Giovanni*, trans. Peter Hebblethwaite, 2nd ed. (Assisi: Citta della Editrice, 1973), pp. 222–223. Hebblethwaite also gives the Latin and Italian on p. 483 of his biography of John.

7. See the author's *Meet Padre Pio: Beloved Mystic, Miracle Worker, and Spiritual Guide* (Cincinnati: Servant, 2001) for testimony of how Pio's superior found this charge spurious.

8. Verified February 25, 2008, by Pio's friary, this intervention was shared by the archbishop with a superior of Pio. I have translated Padre Carmelo da Sessano's testimony. John did permit a much-needed inquiry into conflict between the friary and the hospital Padre Pio had built through donations to serve the area; local women who behaved fanatically, even violently, in their efforts to get the front seats for Pio's Masses, talk to him or gain marks of his favor; and other situations, in all of which the aged saint was victim, not perpetrator.

CHAPTER 16: GO IN PEACE

1. Pope John XXIII, *Pacem in Terris*, April 11, 1963, no. 158, www. vatican.va.

2. Quoted in Benigni and Zanchi, p. 424.

3. Quotes are from Loris Capovilla, "Ultima giorno di Giovanni XXIII," in *Giovanni XXIII*, p. 473.

4. Benigni and Zanchi, p. 428.

5. Benigni and Zanchi, p. 428.

6. Written May 24, 1963, as part of the pope's personal "Act of Faith," quoted in Angelina and Giusepe Alberigo, eds., Giovanni XXIII: Il concilio della speranza (Padua: Edizioni Messaggero Padova, 2000), pp. 252–253.

7. Capovilla, "Ultima giorno," pp. 484–485; Loris Capovilla and Gianni Carzaniga-Pepi Merisio, eds., *Omaggio a Papa Giovanni* (n.p.: S.E.S.A.A.B., 1997), p. 361.

EPILOGUE

1. Back of a photo card sent to the writer.

2. This account appears in my book *Messengers,* now in condensed paperback as *Apparitions of Modern Saints* (Cincinnati: Servant, 2001).

3. Today fewer miracles are required than in John's time, due to the present difficulties of sorting out complex medical treatments from supernatural interventions.

4. A spray had been applied for the public viewing of the pope's body, but this temporary treatment of an unembalmed body can in no way cause incorruptibility. Other bodies buried in the same place and way as John's decayed normally.